GU01017799

Econor

A Mini Text.

A, A/S Level Study and Revision Companion.

ecorp.   Economic Resources Publications.

P.O. Box 147, Durham. DH1, 5WJ.

To Christopher and Philip.

©   **D. J. Buckingham.**

©   **Ecorp.**

First edition published 1993 [ISBN 1-898518-00-9]
Second revised edition 1995 [ISBN 1-898518-01-7]
Reprinted March 1996
Third Edition 1997   [ISBN 1-898518-01-7]
Reprinted November 1998
Revised October 1999

ISBN : 1 - 898518 - 01 - 7
Printed in England.

© **e**corp.   " **Economic Resources Publications.**"

P.O. Box 147, Durham. DH1, 5WJ.

Contents.

Preface.

This booklet is for students studying " A" and " AS" Level Economics, Scottish Higher Grade examinations, and for students studying similar examinations such as first year degree and G.N.V.Q courses. It is intended as an additional study aid which should be used with other economic textbooks, and class notes. The booklet is designed to be a concise and comprehensive guide which will **save** students **valuable revision time.** This booklet also provides students with an easy and quick reference guide to information about the various topics.   It is intended to give students a unique overview of economics .

D. J. Buckingham.   3rd, April 1997

Economics is concerned with how society allocates the use of scarce resources in order to satisfy the greatest number of wants. This introduces two important concepts, **scarcity** and **choice.**

Scarcity means that resources are insufficient or [**finite**] in relation to their productive use [**infinite**]. As resources are scarce society has to make choices in their use. Every society faces 3 basic problems :

• **What to produce.**   [What goods and services to produce and how much.]
• **How to produce.**   [What methods of production to be used.]
• **For Whom**.   [How the goods and services will be distributed.]

Resources.
These are used in the production process and are classified as follows :
• **Land or natural resources.**
The **gifts of nature** of the land, sea, and air. Eg : minerals, fish, trees, climate etc.
• **Capital or man made resources.**
These are used to produce other goods like consumer goods. Eg : machines, plant, tools etc. This is called Productive Capital or Fixed Capital. Capital can also be classifed into the following : Social Capital [schools, hospitals, libraries etc] or Circulating Capital [stocks of raw materials used in production].
• **Labour.**
The collective term given to all human effort in the production process Eg skilled, unskilled, full or part time work, mental and physical effort .
• **Entrepreneurship.**
This is the person or persons that organises, innovates, or is the **risk taker** and puts the other Factors of Production to work.

Economic goods and Free goods.
If resources are scarce a choice has to be made in its use - Opportunity Cost.
Economic Goods. These use scarce resources and therefore have a cost in money terms and an opportunity cost for society [Eg a car].
Free Goods. These have no Opportunity Cost as they are abundant in supply and therefore have no cost in money terms [Eg fresh air].

Opportunity cost.
Scarcity and choice are illustrated by the idea of Opportunity Cost. This is defined as the next best alternative foregone. As resources are scarce it follows that they have alternative uses. Therefore, opportunity cost measures what has to be sacrificed or foregone in order to obtain a desired alternative. The idea of Opportunity Cost is clearly shown by the **Production Possiblity Curve.**

The economic problem.

Production Possibility Curve.

A Production Possiblity Curve shows what society can produce with a given amount
of resources and technology at a given time period.

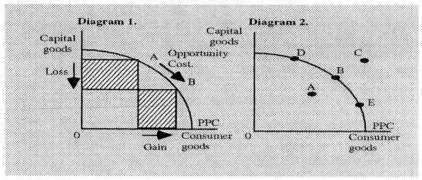

The Production Possibility Curve shows the following points.

• **Diagram 1** illustrates the idea of **Opportunity Cost** [A to B] - the loss of capital
goods for an extra amount of consumer goods.

• **Diagram 2** illustrates the use of productive resources within society.
Point A shows Under utilisation of resources and output below its full potential
[eg: unemployment]. **Point B** shows that resources are fully employed [eg: Full
employment]. It also shows productive and allocative efficiency. While at **point C**
production at this point is impossible with the given level of resources and
technology. **Points D** and **E** show productive efficiency of resources.

The Shape of the Production Possibility Curve.

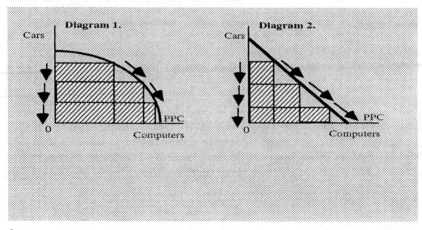

Diagram 1 shows the Production Possiblity Curve concave to the origin. This clearly illustrates that maximum output occurs away from the extreme specialistion i.e at either end of the PPC . As output is increased away from cars to computers the rate of return diminishes as resources are not equally suited to all types of production. Therefore, costs will rise as well as the opportunity cost to society. **Diagram 2** the PPC is represented as a straight line. Here resources are equally efficient in the production of cars or computers. Therefore, as production increases towards computers the opportunity cost to society remains the same.

Shifts in the Production Possibility Curves.

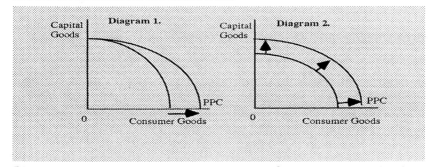

Diagram 1 illustrates an outward movement of the PPC as a result of **specialisation, or a change in technology** in the output of consumer goods, while **Diagram 2** shows an outward movement at both ends of the PPC in other words an increase in both capital and consumer goods. This reflects **economic growth** over time as new resouces are used or discovered combined with improvements in technology, methods of production, education and research.

The Production Possibility curve and Economic Systems.
The production possibility curve can be used to illustrate various combinations of private and public goods under different economic systems.

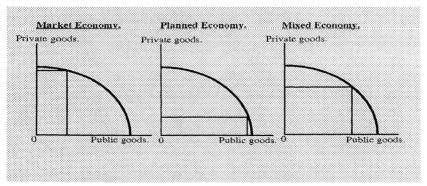

The Economic System.
This is the type of economy which a society adopts to solve the basic economic problem.

The Market Economy.

The key feature of a market economy is lack of government intervention which is referred to as free enterprise or laissez faire economies. Economic decisions on what, how, and for whom to produce are made by market forces (demand and Supply) as resources are allocated through the **price mechanism**.
The main features are as follows :
• Resources are owned and controlled by private individuals.
• Resources are allocated through the price mechanism.
• The profit motive is the main motivating force for entrepreneurs.

Advantages.
• The consumer is king as firms respond to consumer wants.
• The price mechanism ensures that resources are allocated and used most efficiently.
Eg : Those who produce at the lowest cost ensure the greatest profit.
• The price system is **self regulating**.
• The profit incentive encourages innovation, enterprise, and hard work.
• Competition encourages lower prices as firms use the least cost combination of production.

Disadvantages.
• Inequalities in the distribution of income and wealth.
• Those with the ability to buy goods and services are able to influence the allocation of resources. This leaves insufficient resources to meet the needs of the poor as there is little or no provision in regards to the welfare state.
• Prices only reflect private costs and ignore social costs to the community.
Eg : Externalities of production such as pollution, or the impact of production on the environment such as building a road or factory on "green belt" land.
• The profit incentive ignores the production of public goods and the under production of merit goods [ie education and health] and over production of demerit goods [tobacco or alcohol]. Eg : Market failure.
• The lack of government intervention means the economy is very unstable as the level of economic activity fluctuates during the **trade cycle** between slumps and booms. It is left to the market to regulate the level of unemployment and Inflation.

The Planned Economy.

The key feature of this economy is that **resources are owned and controlled by the state** and is referred to as public enterprise. Under this system the decisions of what, how, and for whom are taken by the government (Eg : government committees). The main features are as follows :
• Resources are owned and controlled by the state.
• The state allocates the factors of production, sets production targets and plans.
• The distribution of Income is decided by the government.

Advantages.
These attempt to overcome the disadvantages of the market economy.
• Resources are allocated on social need rather than the purchasing power of individual consumers. Everyone has a fair share of resources.
• Inequalities are reduced by price fixing, restrictions on private ownership, and a progressive taxation system which taxes the rich to provide state benefits for lower income groups.
• Government intervention into the level of economic activity reduces the extremes of the trade cycle such as inflation or massive unemployment.

Disadvantages.
• The lack of incentives such as profit reduces innovation, and enterprise.
• The lack of consumer sovereignty reduces allocative efficiency as planners fail to measure actually real consumer demand. Eg : shortages and surpluses of certain consumer goods as well as an increased emphasis on capital goods.
• Government regulation increases state bureaucracy which will slow down the decision process. Eg : Government committees to approve production plans etc.

The Mixed Economy.

This economic system **embraces both the advantages of the market and planned economies.** Resources are allocated by both the private and public sector.
The main features are as follows :
• The **private sector** controls the majority of resources as the factors of production are owned and controlled by private individuals as goods and services are allocated through the price mechanism. The profit incentive ensures that resources are allocated according to consumer wants [ie consumer is king].
• The **public sector** provides **public goods,** and the means of **regulating the private sector** in the form of Consumer Laws, Health and Saftey Standards, controls on big business through the Monopolies and Mergers Commission, as well as Laws and regulations in regards to externalities by applying the social cost benefit analysis.
It also regulates the economy by curbing inflation, unemployment, encouraging economic growth, as well as ensuring a fair and equal distribution of income and wealth.

The production process involves the use of the factors of production or resources. It also involves the following stages which are associated with the three sectors or industries of the economy.

Primary Production. This involves the extraction of raw materials from nature.

Secondary Production. This converts raw materials into capital or consumer goods. Eg : manufacturing and construction.

Tertiary Production. This involves all services required by primary and secondary industries as well as private individuals.

Factor Combinations or the Least - Cost Combinations.

This means that a firm will organise its **factor inputs** [Land, Labour, and Capital] in such a way as to minimise the cost of production at any given level of output. This is usually expressed as a **ratio** between the productivity of Labour and its price say, compared to the productivity of Capital and its price.

$$\frac{\text{Marginal product of Labour.}}{\text{Price of Labour.}} = \frac{\text{Marginal product of Capital.}}{\text{Price of Capital.}}$$

If the price or productivity changes between Capital and Labour then the firm will adjust these combinations [**factor substitution**] until the marginal product and price ratios are equal again [Eg : If the productivity of Capital increases while all things remain equal, then the firm will reduce the amount of Labour employed until it equals Capital].   However, there are restrictions on factor input combinations as some factor inputs are fixed in supply in the short term.

The Law of Diminishing Returns.

The factors of production used in the production process are distinguished as ;

• **Fixed inputs.** These cannot be easily increased in the short term.
[Eg Land, Skilled Labour, Capital goods].

• **Variable inputs.** These inputs can be increased in the short term.
[Eg unskilled Labour, raw materials and components etc].

The Law states that " **as increasing amounts of a variable factor [Labour] is added to a fixed factor [Capital] output will increase up to a certain point where it will start to diminish or fall.** "   This is illustrated below :

Units of Labour.	Total Output.	Marginal Output.	
1	12	12	Increasing Returns.
2	27	15	
3	47	20	
4	67	20	Constant Returns.
5	83	16	
6	93	10	Diminishing Returns.
7	90	-3	

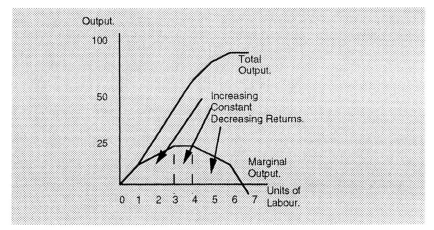

The table and graph above clearly illustrate **three** important points
• **Increasing returns** up to the third worker.
• **Constant returns** between the third and fourth worker.
• **Decreasing returns** between the fourth and seventh worker. The input of the seventh worker has a negative impact on output.
The Law of diminishing returns is important because it measures the **efficiency or productivity of the variable input**. Eg : additional workers operating machinery. It also applies to the **short term** situation.

Returns to Scale.
In the **long term** it is assumed that **all the factor inputs are variable**. In the long term the firm can change it's scale of operation or production. Here economists will measure the firms efficiency by comparing the **factor inputs with the firm's output**.

Measuring changes in production.
• **Total Output.** This is simply total output or production at any given time.
• **Marginal Output.** This is the increase in total ouput as the result of the employment of the additional factor input. Eg : the additional worker employed.
• **Average Output.** This is the total output divide by numbers employed. Eg : Labour.

Costs of Production.
A firms production costs are seen as follows :
• **Accounting Costs.** This is simply all money inputs involved in the production process. Eg : production, administration, financial costs etc.
• **Economic Costs.** This is defined in terms of **Opportunity cost**.

11

Production, Costs, and Returns.

The Firm's Costs.

• **Fixed costs [FC]**. These costs do not change with output whether production is at zero or the firm is operating at full capacity. Eg : rent on premises, machinery.

• **Variable costs [VC]**. These costs are related to the cost of production. Eg : raw materials, cost of labour, power etc.

• **Total costs [TC]**. This is simply Fixed costs + variable costs.

• **Average costs [AC]**. This is Total cost divided by output.

• **Marginal costs [MC]**. This is the additional cost of producing an extra unit of output. Eg : the additions to Total cost as output is increased by additional units.

• **Average Fixed costs [AFC]**. This is fixed costs divided by output. AFC will continue to fall in the short term.

• **Average Variable costs [AVC]**. This is variable costs divided by output.

The Firm's Cost Curves.

The Firm's various cost curves show the relative efficiency of production at each level of output.

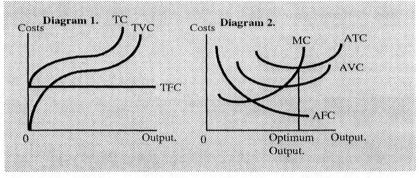

Diagram 1 clearly shows the effect of the **combination of the factor inputs** on Output. If the inputs are inefficiently used in the production process then the fixed factor will be either **under** or **over utilised** as TC rises rapidly in relation to output. When the factor inputs are used efficiently then TC rises more slowly in relation to output.

Diagram 2 shows the **optimum level of output** when AC is at its lowest point. At this point the various inputs will be operating at their most efficient, while costs will be at their lowest.

Short term and Long term Cost Curves.

• In the short term at least **one factor input is fixed.** As output increases average costs will fall until the optimum point, after which average costs will rise in accordance to the Law of Diminishing Returns.

• In the long term **all factor inputs are variable**. The firm can change its scale of operations to suit consumer demand. Diagram 2 illustrates the firm's long term cost

12

curve Eg : LAC .   The LAC is sometimes referred to as the **envelope curve** as it
reflects a series of SAC curves each showing different levels of output.   It also
illustrates the **economies** and **diseconomies of scale** on output over time.

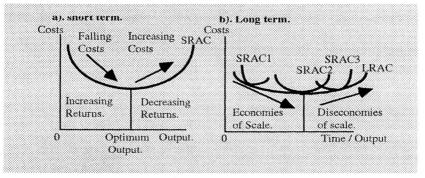

The Firm's revenue.
• **Total Revenue [TR]** is total earnings from its sales. Eg : TR = P x Q.
• **Average Revenue [AR]** is simply Total Revenue divided by Output.
Eg : AR / Q. Average revenue curve is also the firm's **demand curve.**
• **Marginal Revenue [MR]** is the additional revenue from the sale of the last unit.

Economies and Diseconomies of Scale.
Economies of Scale are associated with the **advantages of large scale production**
and reflect the **internal policies** of the firm as output increases. They are as follows
• **Technical Economies.** These are associated with the methods of production.
Eg : specialisation and the division of labour, increased use of capital equipment.
• **Managerial Economies.** The firm can employ specialist managers.
• **Financial Economies.** Easier access to capital, lower rates of interest .
• **Marketing Economies.** The advantages in buying and selling in bulk.
• **Risk -bearing Economies.** A large firm can diversify its operations.

Internal Diseconomies.
This occurs after production increases beyond its optimum output. Inefficiencies
result from its size as the short term average costs start to rise [SAC] Eg : the firm
becomes top heavy [too many managers]. The firm's bureauracy might affect
its business decisions, or industrial relations deteriorate.

External Economies and Diseconomies.
External economies relate to the advantages of the firm's location and are sometimes called the **economies of concentration.** These include; **(i).** A pool of Skilled
labour, **(ii).** Educational and Research facilities, **(iii).** Local component firms
supplying the whole industry etc.   **External diseconomies** are the extra costs
incurred by the concentration of firms, such as rising labour costs, congestion and
pollution etc.

4.   Marginal Utility.

Utility is an economic concept that relates to the amount of **satisfaction** that a consumer gains from the consumption of goods and services. The Law of Diminishing Marginal Utility helps to explain the **downward sloping demand curve.**
This simply states " <u>that as the consumption of a commodity increases, the inczrease in total utility diminishes with each successive unit consumed.</u>"
• <u>Total Utility</u>. This is the **total satisfaction** gained by consuming successive quantities of a good or service.
• <u>Marginal Utility</u>. This is the change in satisfaction from the consumption of each additional unit of a good or service consumed.

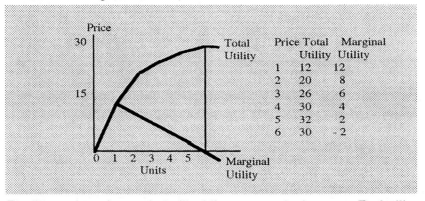

Price	Total Utility	Marginal Utility
1	12	12
2	20	8
3	26	6
4	30	4
5	32	2
6	30	- 2

The diagram shows that marginal utility falls as consumption increases.   Total utility is maximised when marginal utility is zero.

<u>Consumer Equilibrium.</u>   This is a situation where Marginal Utility = Price.   In this situation the rational consumer cannot increase his/her total utility by changing his/her expenditure.   Here **Marginal Utility (MU) = Price (P)**.   The example below shows the consumer equilibrium for more than one commodity.

Eg : <u>Marginal Utility of Good A</u> = <u>Marginal Utility of Good B</u>
    Price of Good A   **Price of Good B.**

If the Price of Good A falls the consumer will simply rearrange his/her expenditure until maximum satisfaction is obtained again [EG : spend more on Good A and less on Good B].   The consumer equilibrium is restored.   This helps to explain the substitution and income effect on demand as a result of a change in price.

14

The indifference curve is based on the notion of **ordinal utility**. This idea is based on preference ranking, and not on any measurable notion of satisfaction gained by the consumption of a good. An indifference curve shows all the combinations or possibilities of two goods whose consumption yields the same total utility.

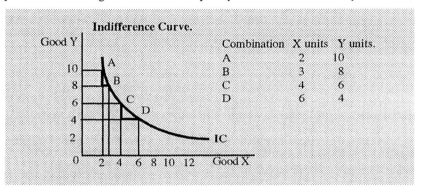

Combination	X units	Y units.
A	2	10
B	3	8
C	4	6
D	6	4

The diagram above shows the combinations of Goods X and Y which are ranked equally by the consumer. The movement along the indifference curve (IC) from A to B shows that only one unit of good X has to be substituted for the loss of the tenth unit of good Y, while two units of good X have to be substituted for the loss of the substitution decreases as more than one good is preferred.

The marginal rate of substitution.
This shows that as more of one good is consumed, its marginal utility diminishes, and therefore less of another good has to be scarificed in order to maintain the same total utility.

The Budget Line.
The budget line shows the possible combinations of goods with a given income.

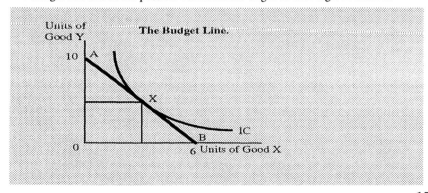

Indifference Analysis.

The **Budget line** is shown by the line **AB.** At the two extremes of the budget line 10 units of good Y, or 6 units of good X could be bought. The consumer will maximise his / or her utility at point X (point of tangency) where the indifference curve touches the budget line.

The consumer equilibrium.
This is when the consumer achieves the maximum utility from the most preferred combinations of goods X and Y, taking into account income and prices.

Factors affecting the consumer equilibrium.
The **two factors** include **a) the substitution effect**, and **b). the income effect.**
The Substitution Effect

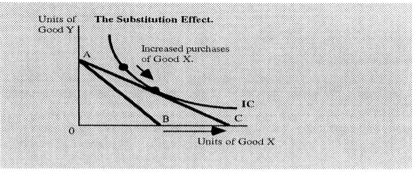

If the price of good X falls and assuming all other factors remain constant (Ceteris Paribus) the budget line will move outwards in favour of good X. The rational consumer will substitute the cheaper good X for good Y. This means the consumer will re-arrange his / her combinations of goods X and Y.
The Income Effect.

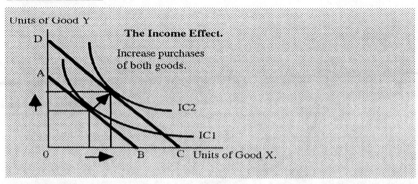

The diagram shows the impact on the budget line from an increase in income. If prices remain constant then an increase in income will move the budget line outwards from AB to CD. This means the **point of tangency** with a higher indifference curve

16

is achieved (IC1 to IC2) and purchases for both goods increase. A reduction in income moves the budget line inwards.

Changes in the consumer equilibrium.

The Price Effect. This is the total effect on consumer equilibrium after considering both the income and substitution effects.
Normal Good. This has a positive income effect as a result of a fall in price.

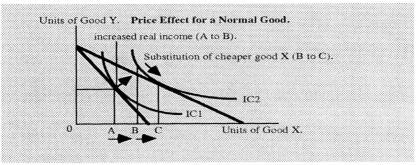

The diagram above clearly shows the effect of a fall in price for a normal good.
• **The income effect** [A to B] shows the budget line moves outwards to a higher indifference curve (IC1 to IC2) .
• **The substitution effect** shows the **movement along IC2.**

Inferior Goods.
This has a negative income effect as a result of a fall in price.

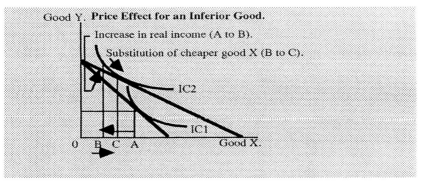

With an inferior good the overall price effect means less is bought from a fall in the price of good X. The increase in real income (A to B) means less is bought of good X as the consumer decides to buy other commodities instead, while the substitution effect (B to C) is weak and fails to outweigh the income effect.
Giffen Good. This a **special type of inferior good.** A fall in price means less of that commodity is being purchased. Eg : a basic necessity - potatoes, bread.

6. Demand, Supply, and Market Equilibrium.

Demand.

Demand, in economics, means **effective demand**, and may be defined as **"the quantity of a commodity which will be demanded at any given price over a given period of time."** The relationship between price and quantity demanded is illustrated by the **demand schedule** and reproduced graphically as a **demand curve.**

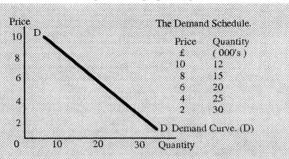

The Demand Schedule.

Price £	Quantity (000's)
10	12
8	15
6	20
4	25
2	30

The **demand curve** normally **slopes downwards** from left to right. It illustrates the basic law of demand, that the quantity demanded will increase as the price falls and vice versa. Eg : When the price falls from £8 to £6 the quantity demanded increases from 15,000 to 20,000 units .

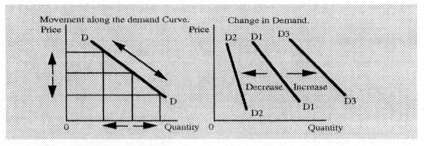

Movement along the demand curve.

A movement along the demand curve **reflects a change in price**. All the conditions that influence demand are held constant [**ceteris paribus**]. This is an important assumption as it allows economists to measure changes in the quantity demanded as a result of a change in price.

Conditions of demand

If any of the conditions of demand changes, it means a shift of the demand curve. The main conditions of demand are classified under the following headings.
• **Disposable income.** An increase in disposable income will generally result in an increase in spending and thereby an increase in demand (and vice versa)
• **Taste or Fashion.** A change in taste or fashion has a powerful influence on demand. This is reinforced by **advertising.**

18

• **Price of other products.**

 Substitutes. Most goods compete with substitutes. A change in the price of one good will affect the demand for it's substitute. Eg : A rise in the price of butter will increase the demand for margarine.

 Complements. These are goods that are in **joint demand.** A rise or fall in the price of one good affects the demand for it's complement. Eg : A rise in the price of cars reduces the demand for petrol, or a fall in the price of cameras increases the demand for films etc.

• **New Products.** Improvements in design, new models, new products, and new inventions will shift demand to the new product, and away from the older model.

• **Population.** Changes in the **total population** or changes in the **age structure** of the population will have a direct impact on demand.

Supply.

Supply is defined as **"the quantities supplied at given prices over a particular period of time."** The market supply curve **slopes upwards** from left to right. The reason for this assumption is that as the price rises, the firm's **profitability** increases. As the price rises firms expand output, while new firms will enter the market. The market supply curve is illustrated below :

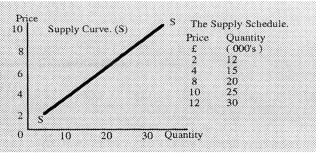

The supply curve illustrates the basic law of supply that **more is supplied at higher prices than lower prices.** Eg: At a price of £4, market supply is 15,000 units but at a higher price of £8 a total of 20,000 units is supplied.

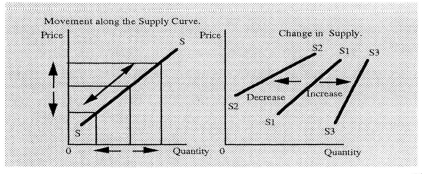

19

Changes in the conditions of supply.
A change in the conditions of supply implies a **complete shift** of the supply curve.

Conditions of supply.
The main conditions that influence supply are as follows:

• **Costs of production.** This is an important element in determining supply. Costs may change for a variety of reasons, i.e. rising **labour costs, raw materials, power** and **transport costs**, and **interest rates** will decrease supply at a given price. On the other hand, the increasing strength of the **exchange rate** will reduce the cost of **imported** raw materials etc. This will increase supply at a given price.

• **Methods of production.** The introduction of **new technology,** new production processes, will increase **productivity.** This means a larger output can be produced with the same labour costs etc. **Supply will move outwards.**

• **Price of other goods.** Changes in the prices of other goods will affect the supply of any commodity whose price does not change.

 Joint supply. The production of one commodity may affect the output of another product Eg : by-product, an increase in beef production will increase leather hides, or a decrease in lamb production will decrease wool output .

 Competitive supply. Some commodities can be used in a variety of production processes. Eg : Steel, Timber, Plastics etc. Therefore, if the price of goods which uses these commodities rises, production and resources will tend to move to those goods which are experiencing higher prices and profits. Eg : Timber to furniture manufacture, to house construction.

• **Taxation.** The government can influence supply directly. The imposition of **indirect taxes (V.A.T & Customs duties)** will increase production costs and **decrease supply,** while **subsidies** and **grants** will reduce costs and **increase supply.**

• **Weather.** This is important for the tourist trade, and agricultural production.

The Market Equilibrium.
This is a state of balance where demand and supply are equal.

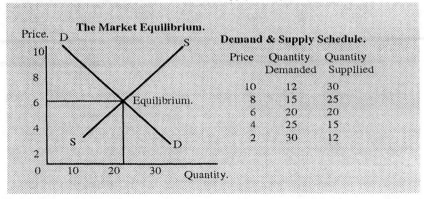

The Market Equilibrium.

Demand & Supply Schedule.

Price	Quantity Demanded	Quantity Supplied
10	12	30
8	15	25
6	20	20
4	25	15
2	30	12

Change in the Equilibrium.
Change in Price.

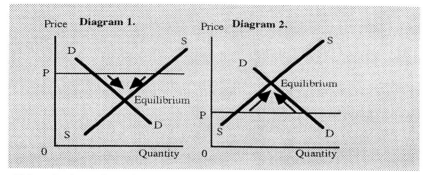

• If the price is set above the equilibrium, supply will exceed demand. The producer will have to eventually reduce his price until the excess stock is sold. Demand and Supply are brought into equilibrium. This is illustrated in **diagram 1**.

• If the price is set below the equilibrium, demand will exceed supply. The **shortage** will force consumers to bid up the price. Demand and Supply will meet at the equilibrium price. This is illustrated in **diagram 2**.

Changes in the conditions of demand and supply.

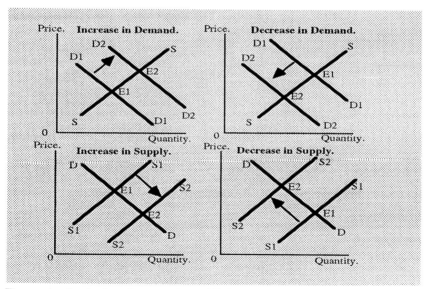

The graphs clearly show that once the equilibrium has been established, a change in the price will occur if there is a change in the **conditions** of **supply** and / or **demand**.

Consumer surplus. This is defined as the difference between what consumers would be willing to pay and the amount actually paid rather than go without the commodity. The shaded area in **diagram (1)** shows the extent of the surplus or extra utility enjoyed by the consumer at the existing market price. This has important implications for both producers [higher prices], and governments [taxes]. The extent of the consumer surplus depends on the market price.
• The lower the market price the larger the amount of the consumer surplus.
• The higher the market price the smaller the amount of consumer surplus.

Producer surplus. This is defined as the difference between the total earnings of suppliers for amounts sold and the actual total costs required to sell the commodity. The shaded area in **diagram (2)** represents additional earnings made at the market price.   The amount of producer surplus depends on the market price.
• The lower the market price the smaller the amount of producer surplus.
• The higher the market price the larger the amount of producer surplus.

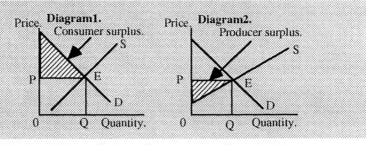

Deadweight or welfare loss. This represents a **loss of allocative efficiency.**

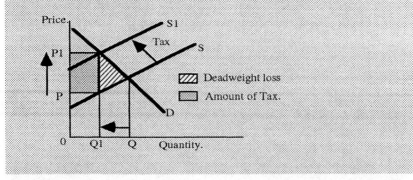

If the government imposes a sales tax like VAT the increase in tax revenue has meant a loss of output with the same resources. Therefore, the deadweight loss represents a loss of allocative efficiency for the community. This means the economy is producing within the Production Possibility curve. The deadweight loss analysis is useful when it's applied to monopolies.

Price Controls. This is when the government sets an artificial price.
• **Maximum prices** protect consumers as the price is set below the market
equilibrium. Eg : basic necessities like bread, milk, public transport etc. Sometimes the government may have to impose regulations, such as rationing in war time
to prevent shortages [ie a **black market price** [BMP]. A government may provide
subsidies [S to S1] to **encourage output** at the lower price.
• **Minimum prices** protect producers as the price is set above the market
equilibrium. This guarantees a reasonable income. However, this usually results
in surplus production. Eg : Farmers in the EU.

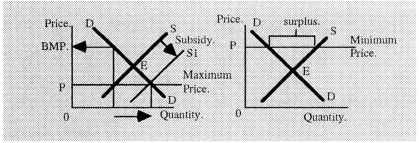

The Labour market.

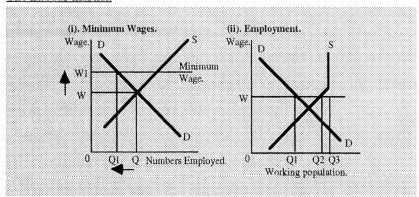

• A government may impose **minimum wage** legislation to protect low paid workers.
However, if the wage is set above the market equilibrium it means a higher cost for
employers who may reduce the numbers employed from Q to Q1. It also encourages
labour substitution with capital.
• This shows that any wage set above the market equilibrium will generate both
involuntary unemployment Q1 to Q2 and **voluntary unemployment** Q2 to Q3.
The area between 0 to Q1 shows the amount of the working population employed.

Agriculture is an industry with thousands of producers, selling homogeneous products for which the world price is the ruling price.   However, farm prices and incomes are subject to high fluctuations unlike manufacturing and the tertiary sector.
The agricultural industry has three closely related features.
• A long term downward fall in prices compared to relative prices in other sectors.
• Prices and incomes have been unstable from year to year.
• Agriculture has been seen as a strategic industry.

The Cobweb Theorem.

This is a dynamic model into the demand and supply analysis.   In this model **time** is included as an **economic variable**.   The Cobweb theorem assumes that **farmers base their supply decisions on prices they received in a previous time period.**
Eg : The market for beef, or carrots.
• It takes time to plant and grow or rear animals for sale.   There is a **time lag.**
• Farmers have to calculate **supply for next season on this year's prices.**   The supply in 1996 is based on the prices in 1995.
• Agricultural products have a relatively **low price elasticity** and changes in supply can cause large movements in price.
• The supply of many agricultural products is subject to **weather** conditions like frosts, floods, and droughts which have an impact on harvests and supply.

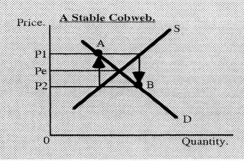

The diagram shows that output is based upon prices received in the previous time period.   Therefore, the price fluctuates from P1 to P2 and output decisions move from A to B which reflects shortages and surpluses of production from one year to another.   **Other types of Cobwebs include :**
A convergent cobweb.   The short term equilibrium price and output moves towards the long term equilibrium.
A divergent cobweb.   The short term equilibrium price and output moves away from the long term equilibrium.

Weaknesses of the Cobweb model.

• In reality farmers use other indicators rather price to form the basis of supply.

• Most governments intervene and regulate agricultural production which reduces the impact of the cobweb.   Eg : C.A.P., or buffer-stock policies, minimum prices etc.

Regulating Agricultural prices.

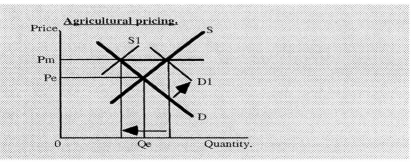

The diagram above shows several options concerning agricultural prices.

By allowing the free forces of the market.   The government could allow the free market to determine the equilibrium price and output [Pe, Qe].   In the long term only the most efficient farmers would remain in production.

By regulating supply .   The government would set minimum price or floor price at Pm.   This may involve buying surplus output.   This would shift the supply curve to the left.   The effect of this measure is to guarantee farmer's incomes as well as supply.

By regulating demand.   The government could increase demand to the right in order to remove any surplus of production [D to D1].   There are two ways in which a government increases demand.

• **Deficiency payments.**   This policy operated in the UK before its entry into the EU and was known as the **"cheap food"** policy.   If prices fell below the agreed floor price, farmers received a subsidy to cover the difference between the floor price and the equilibrium.   This is financed out of general taxation which guarantees farmers incomes and ensures lower prices for consumers

• **Intervention purchases.**   A **"buffer stock"** policy combines both the elements of minimum and maximum pricing as it aims to even out price fluctuations.   The government will determine an intervention price and will buy surplus production, and will release stocks when the price rises above the intervention price.   However, the problems with this policy are that **i).** it is expensive to administer [cost of shortage] and **ii).** if the intervention price is set above the market equilibrium it encourages overproduction.   Eg : beef and butter mountains, and wine lakes in the EU.

Agricultural reforms.

• The EU has introduced **quotas** and **set-aside schemes to reduce supply [S- S1]**.
• The recent reforms within **GATT** will reduce subsidies and agricultural trade barriers allowing more efficient producers from Australia and New Zealand and many third world countries to compete fairly in world markets.

25

Price Elasticity of Demand.

This measures the **degree of responsiveness of the quantity demanded to a change in price.**
The formula for calculating price elasticity of demand is usually expressed as

% change in Quantity demanded.
% change in Price

or $Ed = \dfrac{P}{Q} \times \dfrac{\Delta Q}{\Delta P}$ ΔQ =Change in Quantity.
                       ΔP = Change in Price.
                       P = Original Price.
                       Q = Original Quantity.

It measures the **change in price** between **two points along a demand curve**.
The **coefficient of elasticity** falls into one of the following groups;
• **Infinite Elasticity.** [∞].   This is a perfectly elastic demand curve, and reflects **unlimited** quantity demanded as a result of a change in price.
• **Elastic Elasticity.** [>1]   This reflects a more than proportionate change in quantity demanded to a change in price.
• **Unitary Elasticity.** [1]   A change in price results in an equal proportionate change in quantity demanded.
• **Inelastic Elasticity.** [<1].   This shows a less than proportionate change in quantity demanded to a change in price.
•**Zero Elasticity.** [0].   There is no change in the quantity demanded as a result of change in price.   The demand curve is perfectly inelastic.

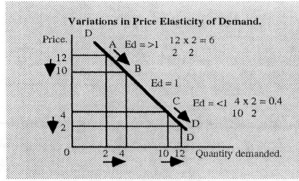

The graph shows the variations in price elasticity along a straight-line demand curve.

The relationship between Elasticity and Total Revenue.

• If demand is **inelastic** a price rise results in an increase in total revenue, while a fall in price results in a decrease in total revenue.
• If demand is **elastic** a price rise results in a decrease in total revenue, while a fall in

26

price results in an increase in total revenue.
• If demand is **unitary** then an increase or decrease in price has no impact on total revenue as it remains the same.

The factors influencing the Price Elasticity of Demand
• **Availability of substitutes.** A product with few close substitutes will be less responsive to a change in price [inelastic] compared to a product with many close substitutes [elastic].
• **The nature of the commodity.** If the good is a necessity it will tend to be inelastic, compared to a luxury good which tends to be more elastic and more responsive to price changes
• **The proportion of income spent on the commodity.** Low priced goods will tend to be inelastic compared to high priced goods which will be more elastic.
• **Habit forming.** Some goods are addictive [cigarettes] and will be inelastic.

Price Elasticity of Supply.
This measures the **degree of responsiveness of the quantity supplied to a change in price.** The formula for calculating price elasticity of supply is expressed as

$$\text{% change in Quantity Supplied.} \quad \text{or} \quad ES = \frac{P}{Q} \times \frac{\Delta Q}{\Delta P}$$
% change in Price.

The elasticities for any given price change are as follows :
• **Zero Elasticity.** [0]. There is no change in the quantity supplied as a result in a change in price. The supply curve is perfectly inelastic.
• **Inelastic Elasticity.** [<1]. This shows a less than proportionate change in quantity supplied to a change in price. The supply curve is relatively inelastic.
• **Unitary Elasticity.** [1] A change in price results in an equal proportionate change in quantity supplied.
• **Elastic Elasticity.** [>1] This reflects a more than proportionate change in quantity supplied to a change in price. The supply curve is relatively elastic.
• **Infinite Elasticity.** [∞]. This is a perfectly elastic supply curve, and reflects unlimited quantity supplied as a result in a change in price.

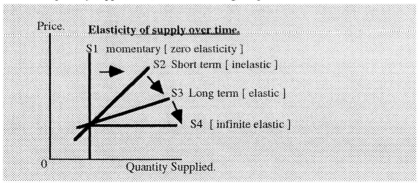

Elasticity of Demand and Supply.

The factors influencing the Elasticity of Supply.

• **The Time Factor.** Supply is going to be more inelastic in the short term, it will be more elastic as resources and stocks can be increased in the long term.

• **Factor mobility.** The greater the mobility of the factors of production the more elastic the supply [vice versa].

• **Entry to the market.** The fewer the barriers to a market the more elastic the supply.

• **Production costs.** If average costs start to rise as a consequence of diminishing returns or diseconomies of scale [vice versa], then supply will tend to be inelastic.

• **Spare capacity.** If firms are operating at full capacity it is impossible to increase supply in the short term. Supply is inelastic [vice versa]

Income Elasticity.

This measures the **responsiveness of demand to changes in income**. This is important for firms and governments responding to changes in consumer incomes. As income rises the proportion of income spent on necessities usually falls, while it increases on luxuries. Therefore, necessities will be inelastic while luxuries will be elastic.

Normal goods. For most necessities and luxury goods the income elasticity will be **positive** as income rises.

Inferior goods. These are goods in which expenditure falls as income rises. A special type of inferior good is called a **Giffen good.**

The formula for calculating income elasticity is as follows;

% Change in quantity demanded.
% Change in income.

The **coefficients** of income elasticity are as follows :
• **Normal Goods : Necessities [0-1] Luxuries [>1]**
• **Inferior Goods : [<1]**

Cross Elasticity.

This measures the responsiveness of demand for one good to a change in price of another good.

The formula for calculating Cross Elasticity is as follows :

% change in quantity of Good X
% Change in Price of Good Y

The **coefficients** of Cross Elasticity are :
• Positive for Substitutes [>1]
• Negative for complements [<1]

28

10.   Markets and Competition.

There are basically two types of market situations.
Perfect Competition.   Firms have no influence in the workings of the market.
Firms are " price takers " and only respond to consumer demand.
Imperfect Competition.   This market situation covers monopoly, monopsony,
duopoloy, oligopoly, and monopolistic competitors.   In this type of market the firm
is more of a " Price maker " and can therefore influence the market price.

Perfect Competition.
Conditions of Perfect Competition.
• A large number of buyers and sellers.
• Buyers and sellers have perfect knowledge of goods and prices in the market.
• Perfect mobility of the factors of production which respond immediately to chang-
ing market conditions.
• Freedom of entry as firms can enter and leave the industry.
• Homogeneous product as all firms in the industry produce and sell an identical
product which is not differentiated by the use of advertising and brand names.

The advantages of perfect competition can be summarised as follows.
• Lower prices by increased competition.
• All firms in the long term earn normal profits.
• Its impossible to control the market by restrictive trade agreements and cartels
which prevent consumer exploitation.

Imperfect Competition.
Conditions of Imperfect Competition.
In reality most firms operate under one of the following markets which do not
comply with all the conditions of perfect competition.
Monopoly.
This is a situation where the monopolist is the sole supplier or seller in the market.
The monopolist can increase the price or restrict output of his product in order to
increase sales revenue as the demand curve is less elastic.

Types of Monopoly.
• **Pure or absolute monopoly.** No close substitutes.
• **Technological monopolies.** High capital costs, eg telecommunications.
• **Natural monopolies.** There are two types :
   i).   Ownership of mineral resources [gold in South Africa].
   ii).   Statutory monopolies established by governments [eg the public utilities].
• **Artificial monopolies.** These are deliberately created by firms in order to make
abnormal profits. Eg : Take overs, amalgamations, or cartels.

Advantages of monopolies.

These can be summarised under the following headings
• Encourage Economies of Scale.
• Rationalisation of resources within the industry.
• Continuity of production as the monopolist has the resources to maintain output during times of recession.
• Monopolies may be justified as they reduce wasteful duplication, and provide essential services as in the public utilities [service before profit].

Disadvantages of monopolies.
• Higher prices and reduced output to maintain higher profits.
• Lack of innovation and incentive to improve products and production methods in order to reduce costs and prices.
• Less variety of goods from less competition.
• The loss of allocative efficiency as resources are not used as productively as under perfect competition..

Controlling Monopolies.
The monopolist power can be restricted by the following measures :
• **Government intervention.** A government can use a variety of methods which include, price controls, fiscal measures, Consumer laws; the threat of nationalisation or investigation by the Monopolies and Mergers Commission.
• **Market influences.** Too high prices and profits may encourage new firms to enter the market, or force buyers to look for alternatives or substitutes.

Monopsony. This is a sole buyer of goods or services. [Monopoly employer].

Duopoly This is a market controlled by two suppliers.

Oligopoly
This is a market dominated by a few firms [eg Banks, Oil companies]. The main feature of this market is that the firms engage in **non-price competition** as a price war only benefits the consumer and means loss of profits.

Monopolistic competition.
This is a market situation which has a large number of firms producing a similar but differentiated product. Each firm uses advertising, packaging, or brand names to compete with its rivals. This takes the form of **non- price competition.**
These are marketing policies that do not involve price reductions, but involve Product differentiation. These include, product variation through design changes and styles, the use of brand names and logos and packaging, after sales servicing, promotions by the use of sponsorships etc. These methods are clearly illustrated in the car, electrical appliances and financial services industries etc.

The Equilibrium of the Firm.
The firm is in equilibrum when **M.R. = M.C.**

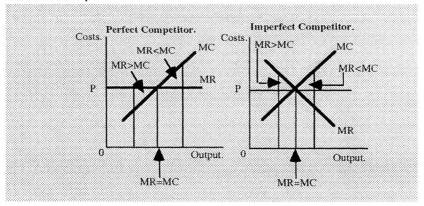

The Profit maximisation theory.
• If **MR>MC** , then the last unit is adding more to revenue than cost. The firm will increase output to maximise profit [to gain extra sales revenue from last unit].
• If **MR<MC**, then the last unit of output is adding more to costs than revenue. The firm will reduce output in order to maximise profits. [reduce loss of last unit]
• If **MR=MC**, then the last unit of output equals the revenue and cost of producing that unit of output. At this point the firm maximises profit and will be in equilibrium.

Perfect Competitor.
Short term situation. Under perfect competition firms earning abnormal profits will attract other firms into the market.
Long term situation. As new firms enter the market existing producers will expand output for a share of the abnormal profits. Evenually, all firms in the industry earn normal profits as the abnormal profits will be competed away. There is no incentive to increase or decrease output.

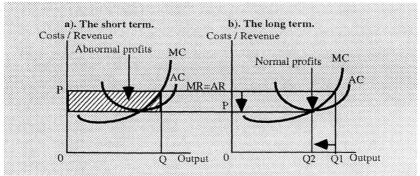

31

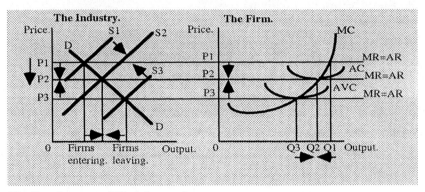

The Break even and Shut down prices.

• The firm's **break-even price** is where the firm earns **normal profit.** At this point
P = AR = AC, or TR = TC. This is also the **firm's long term** equilibrium.
• The firm's **shut-down price** is where P = AVC. At this point the firm will be
making a **loss** or **subnormal profit.** However, the firm will continue production in
the **short term** as long as the price is above AVC. This is because **fixed costs** have
to be paid regardless of the level of output. As long as the price is above AVC its
running costs will be covered. P = AVC, or TR =TVC. If the price falls below
AVC the firm will leave the industry or stop production.

Derivation of the Firm's Supply Curve.

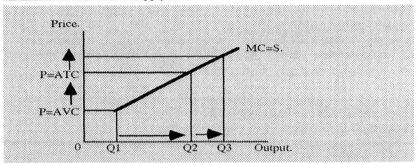

In the **short term** the supply curve of the firm is the MC Curve above the point
where the **Price equals AVC.** As the price rises above AVC the firm's profitablity
increases and output expands. In the **long term** the supply curve of the firm is
where P=MC=AC.

Profit.

• **Normal profit.** Is the **minimum return** sufficient to keep the entrepreneur
employed in the business. This is the entrepeneur's transfer earnings.

• **Abnormal profit**. This is **surplus earnings** to normal profit. This could be referred to as economic rent.
• **Subnormal profit.** This is less than normal profit, the firm makes a **loss** .

Monopoly Equilibrium.
Unlike perfect competition the monopolist is able to prevent new firms entering the industry by technical or statutory barriers etc. If the monopolist is making abnormal profits in the short term they are likely to persist in the long term. However, the monopolist will not always make abnormal profits as it will depend on the relationship between consumer demand [AR] and production costs.

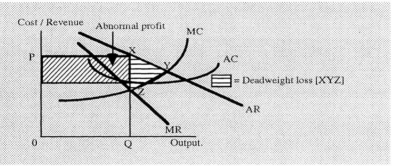

Monopoly and Allocative Efficiency.
Under perfect competition resources are allocated according to consumer demand. However, the monopolist can restrict output and push up the price to earn abnormal profit. This means a re-allocation of resources to some less desired point on the Production Possibility Curve. The **socially desirable equilibrium** which achieves the allocative efficiency under perfect competition is at **point Y**, or where P[AR] = MC or D=S. Deadweight loss will be zero. Under monopoly the **loss of allocative efficiency** is represented by the area of **XYZ [deadweight loss]**.
The monopolist is also technically inefficient as it has little incentive to produce at its lowest cost where MC = AC.

Monopoly and Government intervention.

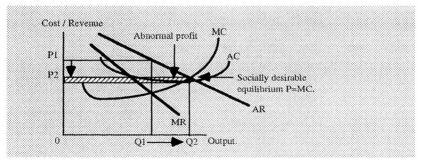

33

The government can regulate a monopoly by the introduction of **price controls.**
This reduces the price to the consumer [P1 to P2], while increasing output from
OQ1 to OQ2.   The benefit for the community is an increase in **allocative efficiency**
as the **welfare loss** is eliminated.   P = MC.

Mark-up pricing. The monopolist has the ability to maintain the Price > MC in the
long term.   Under perfect competition the Price =MR = MC in the long term.
Therefore, the mark-up of P>MC in long term depends on the following factors :
• The ability to **exclude competitors** entering the industry.
• The **elasticity of demand** for its product.

Price discrimination. The monopolist is able to charge consumers different prices
in seperate markets for the same product.   The costs of production remain the same
in both markets.   Therefore, the monopolist is able to increase profit maximisation.

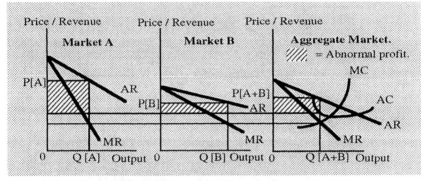

Profit maximisation is achieved when MR = MC.   In **market A** the demand is less
elastic compared to **market B** which is more **elastic.**   By dividing the market the
monopolist will earn a higher income than by charging one aggregate price.
If demand was inelastic then marginal revenue would be negative.

Monopolistic Competitors.

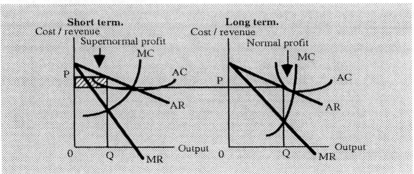

34

Monopolistic competitors earning abnormal profits in the short term will attract new firms into the industry. The level of abnormal profits will be competed away until all firms earn normal profits in the long term as shown in **diagram b.** The ability of firms to maintain a level of abnormal profit depends on how successful they are to **differentiate** their product through the use of brand names, advertising, etc.

Oligopoly.

Features of oligopoly.
• Supply is controlled by a few firms.
• Firms are interdependent.
• There are barriers to entry as firms earn abnormal profits in the long term.

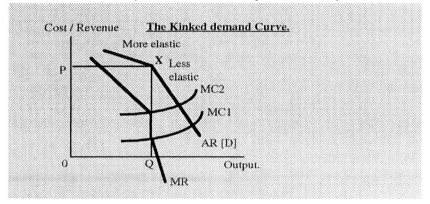

The **kinked Demand Curve** helps to explain price rigidity that occurs under Oligopoly. The market price will be fixed at point X.
• As demand is more elastic above point X any price rise will result in a fall in total revenue as consumers switch to rival products.
• As demand is less elastic below point X and a fall in price will mean a fall in total revenue. A price war will develop. Therefore, competition will take the form of **non-price marketing strategies** or **product differentiation** in order to increase market share.
• Prices remain stable because of the **discontinuity** of the MR curve. Changes in costs between MC1 and MC2 will not affect the profit maximising level of output or the profit maximising price.
Forms of Oligopolistic competition.
a). Competitive Oligopoly.
Firms will use forms of "**Non-Price Competition**". This involves selling a differentiated product which takes the of Advertising, marketing, and packaging competition where the firm uses a variety of advertising campaigns to promote a particular brand. The promotion of a particular brand is a key feature of this type of market. It is important because it helps to give a product an identity and helps to

35

create consumer loyalty.   It makes demand less elastic.   A Mars bar, or Kellogg's corn flakes or a Ford car are unique products.   Higher priced branded goods will sell far better than lower priced unbranded products.   Other aspects of non-price competition include warranties and guarantees, after sales service, and design.   Therefore, firms will decide on the "marketing mix" which best suits their products, or marketing strategy.   This is referred to as the "4 P's".

b). Collusive Oligopoly

Firms operating under a **Collusive Oligopoly** will often benefit if they collude. This involves making agreements amongst themselves in order to restrict competition and maximise profits.   Eg: OPEC illustrates a cartel of Oil producers.   Other examples of collusion include collusive tendering, dominant and barometric price leadership.

Forms of pricing under oligopoly
Price leadership.

This is where one firm in an oligoplistic market is accepted as the market leader in affecting changes in prices.   This is referred to as " **parallel pricing**" as rivals follow suit to the market leader.   A firm may act as a **barometric leader** [employs the best accountants, sales staff], while in other cases the firm may be the **dominant leader** in the industry as the smaller firms are unwilling to challenge its price.

Limit pricing

This is where a firm sets a price low enough to deter new firms from entering the market.   The extent of the limit price depends on the level of barriers in the market.

Price discrimination

This is where a firm charges different prices for the same product to different segments of the market.   There must be no seapage between markets,

Skimming or creaming.

This is pricing to maximise profit.   A firm may charge a high price initially but it may be reduced later as rival products come onto the market.

Predatory pricing

This where a firm sets a low price in the attempt to force rivals out of the market. Aggressive price wars are an example of this type of pricing strategy.

Games Theory

An important feature of Oligopoly is interdepence.   The actions of one large firm will affect all other firms within the industry.   The games theory attempts to analyse the behaviour of firms as a game played between competitors.   Each firm is aware of the effects of its rival competitors' actions and tries to anticipate what they will do. This means no firm never achieves its optimal strategy.   The firms behaviour depends on the actions of other firms within the industry.

The Zero-sum game.

This is the worst extreme of the games theory.   This means the gain by one firm is exactly offset by the loss of another firm. Eg: If one firm increases market share by 5% it will be at the expense of another firm.

11. Theory of a Contestable Market

A contestable market is where there is **"freedom of entry to an industry and where the costs of exit are low"**.

Assumptions
- The number of firms in any particular industry can vary.
- There is both freedom of entry and exit from the market.
- Firms compete with each other, and do not collude to fix prices.
- Firms are short term profit maximisers. Eg : producing where MR=MC.
- Firms may produce homogeneous products, or branded goods.
- There must be perfect knowledge in the industry.

Features of a contestable market.
- **Abnormal and normal profit.**

Firms earning abnormal profits will attract new firms into the market. In a contestable market all firms will earn normal profit in the long term. Firms earning subnormal profits will leave the industry.
- **Freedom of entry and exit.**

The ability for firms to enter and leave an industry is critical to the theory of a contestable market, rather than the number of firms in the industry.

Entry costs.

In some markets barriers are **"natural"** - [innocent entry barriers] such as a natural monopoly - railtrack, the national grid [very high fixed or capital costs]. This makes it difficult for new firms to enter the industry.

Exit costs or sunk costs.

If exit or sunk costs are low then it is possible for firms to enter the market without great loss on exit. Eg: The **"hit and run"** firm. A new firm could enter a market, earn a profit, before being forced out by an established competitor. Therefore it is worthwhile for the firm to enter the market.
- **The threat of potential competition.**

Firms earning "abnormal profit" are dependent on barriers to entry. In a contestable market existing firms will have reduced prices [limit pricing] in order to stop a "hit and run" firm becoming established in the market.
- **Increasing efficiency.**

In a contestable market all firms will earn "normal profits" in the long term where P=MC=AC. Therefore, firms will both be allocative, and productively efficient.

Conclusion.
The emphasis of government Competition policy since the 1980's is to try and make individual markets more contestable. This forms the basis of many supply-side policies which include privatisation and deregulation.

12. Competition Policy.

Competition policy aims to make markets are more contestable.

• **Monopolies & Mergers Commission.**
The MMC will investigate cases of **dominant firm monopolies**, where a **firm controls 25% of the output of an industry** (national or local monopolies). This will be investigated to determine if the monopoly is in the **Public interest**.

Types of monopoly
A scale monopoly is when a firm controls 25% of the market for a particular good or service.
A complex monopoly is where two or more firms together have a 25% market share in order to restrict competition. Eg : As a result of a merger or takeover.

• **Restrictive Practices Court.**
Restrictive Practices is an agreement between firms in respect of price or conditions of supply which will restrict competition.

• **The Director General of Fair Trading** is appointed by the government and is responsible for co-ordinating competition and consumer protection policy and advising the Secretary of State.

• **Consumer watchdog.** Agencies such as Oftel, Ofwat, Offer, Ofgas, Ofrail, have the powers to ensure that the privatised utilities maintain minimum standards of service and prices.

Privatisation and Deregulation.
This is the transfer of public resources to the private sector plus various supply-side measures to reduce barriers to competition.

Forms of Privatisation.
• **The sale of Nationalised industries.** This involves the sale of the ownership of various government businesses. Eg : British Airways, British Gas, British Telecom.
• **Deregulation.** This involves increasing competition and reducing restrictions within certain industries. Eg ;Telecommunications, Financial deregulation etc.
• **Contracting out.** Where government services are contracted out to the private sector by tender. Eg: School and Hospital cleaning.
• **Commercialisation or marketisation**. The government encourages the private sector to compete directly with the public sector-private education, health, pensions.

Reasons for privatisation.
• **To increase efficency.** Competition encourages cost savings and innovation.
• **To increase competition.** They respond to the needs of the consumer.
• **To increase private capital and expertise.** Privatisation allows these businesses to raise private capital and recruit managers from the private sector.
• **To raise government revenue.** It provides government income.
• **To reduce the PSBR.** It reduces the level of government borrowing.

Arguements against privatisation.
• **Strategic reasons.** Many industries are important to the economy. Under public ownership supply is guaranteed. EG : British Airways, British Steel..
• **Natural Monopolies.** The break-up of a natural monopoly may increase costs.
• **Private Monopolies.** These monopolies are only answerable to its shareholders.

38

Small firm.

There is no clear definition of a small firm and this will vary depending on the type of industry being examined.   However, generally the **Bolton Report** which was updated by the **Wilson Committee** stated that a small firm was one that employed less than 200 people and had three additional characteristics - **(i)** a small market share, **(ii).** was not part of another organisation or business, and **(iii).** its owners took an active interest in the business.   The **Companies Act of 1985** gives an alternative definition from an accounting perspective.   A business is considered small if it satisifies any two of the following,

   i). A turnover of less than £2 million.

   ii). An average of 50 employees or less.

 iii). Has net assets under £975,000.

Ways of measuring the size of firms.
a). Turnover, **b).** Market share, **c).** Number of employees, **d).** Capital employed.

Reasons for survival of small firms.
Small firms survive for many reasons.
• **Entrepeneurial spirit.** Individuals are motivated by self employment.
• **Lack of finance.** Small firms lack the capital to expand into larger businesses.
• **Limited market demand.** Small businesses offer personal services, specialised products, or **niche** markets.
• **Policy of large firms.** Large firms may order components, or sub-contract work to smaller firms.
Small firms are important for the economy because they tend to be more labour intensive, and some will grow into larger businesses.   It has been estimated that small firms accounted for 25% of total employment in 1990, or 20% of GNP.

Growth of Firms.

There are **two ways** in which firms can grow and expand.
• **Internal growth** occurs by " **ploughing profits back** " into the business.   This is usually associated with **"economies of scale."**   As firms grow in size they will experience a fall in average costs.   Economies of scale may be **"internal"** economies which may be categorised as follows : technical, marketing, managerial, risk bearing, or financial economies, or **"external"** economies which are associated with the advantages of its location Eg : pool of skilled labour, research falicities etc.
• **External growth** occurs when one firm combines with another firm either by amalgamation or merger.   This is considered a cheaper option than investing in new plant and capital.

   i).   Take-over. Is where firms are joining together not on equal terms and the firm being taken over is against the offer.

   ii).   Merger. Is where firms amalgamate voluntarily and combine their assets to form a single business.

iii). Holding Company. Is when a company acquires 51% of its voting shares. They become a subsidiary of the holding company.

Types of mergers.
Expansion by merger or amalgamation is usually referred to as integration.
• **Horizontal mergers** occur at the same stage of production [eg : two breweries].
• **Vertical mergers** occur at different stages of production. There are two types ;
  i). **Backward vertical merger**-to ensure its **source of supply.**
  [eg ; brewery buys a hops farm].
  ii). **Forward vertical merger** to ensure a **market outlet**.
  [eg : brewery buys a Public House].
• **Lateral mergers** occur between firms using similar production methods to produce similar commodities. [eg : A brewery and a distillery]
• **Conglomerate mergers** occur between firms producing goods not directly related to one another. { eg : brewery and a computer company.].

Reasons for Mergers
a). Economies of Scale, **b).** Rationalisation, **c).** Diversification, **d).** Increase market share, and **e).** Protection against foreign competition.
If a proposed merger is considered against the public interest the Secretary of State for Trade and Industry can refer the merger to the **Monopolies and mergers Commission.**

Concentration ratios.
The merger boom of the 1960's and 1970's has increased concentration ratios in many industries. Concentration ratios measure the sales of the three or five largest firms in a particular industry. The greater the concentration ratio the greater the possibility of a monoploy or oligopoly situation. It also indicates the economies of scale which will reduce competition from smaller firms. Eg : In 1990 the 5 firm concentration ratio was 9.9% in Machine hand tools, compared to 87.3% for Motor vehicles and engines, and 99% in the Tobacco industry.

Multinational Corporations.
A Multinational Corporation is a business which operates on an international basis. These firms include Ford, Nissan, Shell and B.P, IBM, and ICI. Multinationals exist for many reasons which include **a).** To avoid monopoly legislation in its home country, **b).** To increase market share, **c).** To obtain the benefits of cheap labour and raw materials.
The rapid rise of Multinationals over recent decades has provided advantages and disadvantages. Supporters of Multinationals argue that they increase efficiency as they rationalise resources, while critics say that they are too powerful and gain an unfair advantage particularly in developing countries.

40

14. Market Failure.

Market Failure.
This is when the price mechanism fails to allocate resources efficiently . This may justify state intervention.

Reasons for State Intervention.
The government has many different roles in the economy.
• **Regulatory role.** To provide a basic legal system to ensure that the market system operates effectively. Eg : Property rights, Consumer Laws, Health & Safety regulations, Company Acts etc.
• **Allocative role.** The provision of public goods and services which the private sector is unwilling to provide. Eg : Education, Heath.
• **Distribution role.** To ensure a fair and equal share of resources by taxing those on higher incomes and providing welfare benefits for those on lower incomes.
• **Stabilisation role.** To regulate the economy by curbing inflation, promoting employment, and economic growth [movements of the trade cycle].

Market Allocation.
In order to achieve the efficient allocation of scarce resources the market system must operate efficiently. This is best illustrated by the Production Possibility Curve.

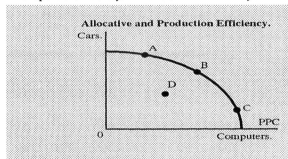

• **Production Efficient.** This is achieved by the Least Cost Combination . Points A, B, and C on the Production Possibility Curve reflect production efficiency. Point D shows that production is inefficient or within the Production Possibility Curve.
• **Allocative Efficient.** This occurs where output best meets consumer's demands. At point B production is both allocative and production efficient. This is sometimes referred to as economic efficiency as price = MC in all industries.
• **Equity.** The market system rewards some factors of production (ie Labour) with higher incomes than other factors. As incomes are used to buy goods and services the market determines for whom to produce. The government may have to intervene to reduce any unfairness.

Internal and External costs , and benefits.

• **The Marginal Benefit Curve (MB)** represents the demand curve as it shows the willingness to pay or Marginal Utility represents the **internal benefits** enjoyed by consumers.

• **The Marginal Cost Curve (MC)** represents the **private cost** the firm has to pay in order to produce each additional unit. This is the **internal costs** of production.

• The **Marginal Social Benefit Curve (MSB)** represents the private benefit plus the **spillover benefits** enjoyed by third parties from consuming an extra unit of a good or service. This shows the external benefits enjoyed by the community which are not paid by those who receive them.

Eg : The benefits of a by-pass, or an orchard situated next to a number of bee-hives.

• The **Social Marginal Cost Curve (SMC)** is the private cost plus the **spillover cost** of producing an extra unit of a good or service imposed on third parties. This shows the external cost for society. Eg : Dumping waste into a river.

The Social Equilibrium.

The **social equilibrium** for society is where **MSC = SMB**. It represents the maximising net benefits for society as utility less costs are achieved where **SMB = SMC**. This takes into account the full social cost and social benefit of resource allocation.

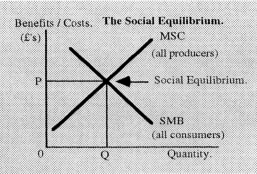

Externalities.

These are the **spillover effects of consumption or production on third parties for which no compensation is paid.** They show the external cost or benefit which the market system fails to take into account. These can be or negative or positive.

Eg : Pollution, congestion, or water purification.

• **Negative Externalities**. These are **spillover costs** or side effects of production [eg air pollution, polluted rivers etc]. This is shown as a **welfare loss** [XYZ].

• **Positive Externalities.** These are **spillover benefits** enjoyed by the community as the result of production [eg less air pollution as commuters use public transport.]. This is shown as a **welfare gain** [XYZ].

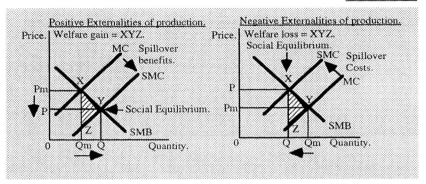

Cost-Benefit Analysis.

This calculates the full economic cost and benefit of a particular economic activity. It involves assessing the private costs and negative externalities of production with its private benefits and positive externalities.

Eg : A motorway, building a factory, or houses on the greenbelt land etc.

Public Goods.

The market system will not produce goods that are not profitable. Public goods fall into this category as they display two basic characteristics which together make them unprofitable.

Characteristics of Public Goods.

• **Non-Rivalry.** This means once the good is supplied to one consumer there is little or no additional cost in supplying to others. In other words a person's consumption of a public good does not reduce its benefit to others.

• **Non-Excludablity.** This means that it cannot be supplied to one consumer without supplying it to others. Other individuals cannot be stopped from benefiting from its use. Eg : Street-lighting, Defence.

Pure Public Goods.

They display **total non-rivalry** and **total non-excludability**.

Free Riders.

The problem of non-excludability creates the problem of free-riders. A free rider is able to consume and enjoy the benefits of its use of a good without paying for it. Eg : Ships using the benefits of a lighthouse.

Merit Goods

This is a good which is considered good for people. Such goods include Education, the wearing of seat-belts, Health-care and they may be **undervalued** by consumers. To encourage consumption the government may provide subsidies, or provide them at no cost to the consumer.

43

Market Failure.

Demerit Goods.

These are cosidered bad for people. These include smoking, drinking and may be
overvalued by consumers. The government may **impose taxes** in order to discourage consumption, or ban them completely as with drugs.

Efficiency and Equity of the market.

Markets must not only be allocatively efficient, but output and resources must also be
distributed fairly within society.

Equity and Equality.

• **Equality.** Disposable incomes must be the same for all in society.
• **Equity.** The distribution of income must be considered to be fair. This involves
value judgements on what is considered to be fair.
Eg : Incentives, equality of opportunity, welfare safety net, distribution of income.

Absolute and Relative Poverty

Absolute poverty exists when individuals do not have the resources to consume the
necessities to maintain life, whereas relative poverty is defined as relative to existing
living standards for the average individual or household. Therefore, it is more
subjective and will always be present in society.

Problems of measuring Income distribution.

• Problems of measuring an individuals income.
• Household income as opposed to individual income.
• Income earned over a full life time.

Ways of measuring income distribution.

Lorenz Curve. This measures the cumulative % of households and their
cumulative % of income and wealth.

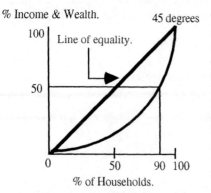

% Income & Wealth.

The graph shows two key points :
a). The Line of equality
shows an equal distribution
of income & wealth, as 50%
of households own 50% of the
income & wealth.
b). The Lorenz curve in this
example shows that 90% of
Households own 50% of the
income & wealth, or alternatively
10% of households own the
remaining 50%.

Disposable income indices.

44

The Simple Circular Flow Model.
The circular flow diagram illustrates a simple model of the economy.
• **Real flow.** This shows the **physical flow** of economic resources [land, labour, capital, and enterprise] which are owned by households used to produce goods and services by firms.
• **Money flow.** This shows a **monetary flow** of income which is generated from use of factor resources [rent,wages interest, and profit] which is used to buy consumer goods and services fom the producers or firms.

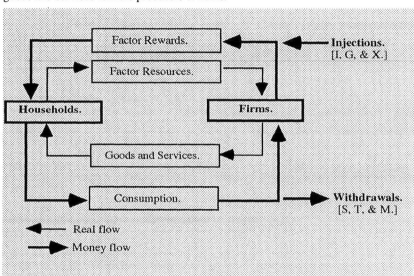

Money and income.
Money is a stock of pounds at any given time, while income is a flow generated out of the productive use of a resource in the circular flow.

National Income.
National income **measures the value of goods and services that are produced in the economy during a given time period** [ie a year]. This is usually expressed as an economic indicator of **G.D.P,** or **G.N.P.**
• **Gross Domestic Product.** [**G.D.P.**].
This measures the total economic activity within the U.K.
• **Gross National Product.** [**G.N.P.**].
This measures the total activity of U.K. citizens around the world.
• **Net Property income from abroad.**
This is the balance or difference of income from overseas assets owned by British citizens and payments to foreigners who own assets inside the U.K.

National Income.

• **Net National Product. [N.N.P.]**
This makes an allowance for **capital depreciation** or replacement investment of plant, machinery, and equipment.   Eg : wear and tear, or become obsolete.
Therefore, G.N.P. - depreciation [Capital consumption] = N.N.P.
• **Residual error.** This is a **balancing item** which allows for discrepancies in the collection of data as collected from different sources.   It may be positive or negative as income and expenditure methods of national income accounting must be identical in theory.   This is sometimes referred to as " **statistical discrepancy.**"
• **Stock appreciation.**   This is an increase in the value of inventories as a result of inflation and is not an increase in output.

The circular flow also gives a basic identity of national income accounting :

National Income = National Output = National Expenditure.

This shows that the total value of goods and services produced is equal to the total factor incomes generated which is equal to the total expenditure on those goods and services.   These three methods of calculating national income are used in the government statistics.

Measuring National Income.
Income Method.
This measures the **incomes** of all individuals and firms [rent, wages, interest, and profit.], plus the trading surplus of the public sector.
This is equal to **total domestic income at factor cost.**

Adjustments to the Income Method.
• **Transfer Payments.** These include social security and unemployment benefits, state pensions, interest on the national debt etc .   These incomes are not productive and are simply transferred from one section of the community to another.   They are excluded.
• **Undistributed profits and surpluses.** Not all profits are distributed to shareholders, as some are retained for future investment.   Therefore, it includes Gross profit.
• **Stock appreciation.**   A deduction must be made to an increase in the value of stock as a result of inflation.
• **Statistical discrepancy.** This allows for errors in the calculation of national income figures.
• **Net property income from abroad.** This adds income from overseas assets and converts GDP to GNP at factor cost.

Output Method.

This adds up the total **value of output** in the economy. This gives the value of
Gross domestic product at factor cost.

Adjustments to the Output Method.
• **Double counting.** This is referred to as the value added method as output must
only include the **value** of output at each stage of production. This stops items being
counted more than once.
Eg : Steel in a car. Steel output at the steel-mill, and in a car assembly plant would
be added twice. Therefore, the value of inputs [purchases] is deducted from the
value of outputs [sales]. This is expressed as Sales - Purchases = Value added
output.
• **Public goods.** Services like education, health care, and defence are provided by
the state and not through the market and therefore have no market price. They are
measured at factor cost [ie the wages of teachers, doctors etc.].
• **Payments in Kind.** This includes vegetables grown in the garden; D.I.Y. improvements, car repairs are not included as they have no market price. This is a real
problem in developing countries where subsistence farming is common and based on
a family unit.
• **The hidden economy.** This is the unrecorded production as a result of criminal
activity or jobs undertaken on " cash-in-hand " basis .
• **Exports and imports.** Exports add to the value output produced in the U.K.,
while imports are deducted as they add to the value of another economy.
• **Statistical discrepancy.** This allows for errors in the calculation of national
income figures.
• **Net property income from abroad.** This adds value of output from overseas
assets and converts GDP to GNP at factor cost.

Expenditure Method.

This is the **total spending** at market prices on all goods and services within the
economy. This gives a value of total domestic expenditure at market prices.
The expenditure method is sometimes expressed as **C + I + G + (X - M)**.

Adjustments to the Expenditure Method.
• **Consumers expenditure.** Only new expenditure [current expenditure] is included, otherwise items like second hand cars would be counted twice.
• **General government final consumption.** This only includes current expenditure
by Central and Local government. It excludes investments and transfer payments
such as grants and subsidies.
• **Gross investment.** This includes gross domestic fixed capital formation
[eg machinery, equipment etc], and physical increases in stocks in work in progress.
• **Exports and Imports.** Expenditure on exports is included, while imports are
deducted.
• **Statistical discrepancy.** This allows for errors in the calculation of figures.

47

• **Net property income from abroad.** This adds net expenditure from overseas assets and converts GDP to GNP.

Useful National Income equations.
GNP = GDP + Net property income from abroad.
NNP = GNP - Capital consumption [depreciation].
Net Investment = Gross investment - depreciation or replacement investment.
Factor cost = Market prices - Indirect taxes + subsidies.

Importance of National Income.
• ts a measure of living standards.
• It helps to compare living standards between countries.
• It shows the allocation of resources within the economy.
• It provides data for future government planning.
• It is a measure of economic growth.

Problems of National Income accounts.
• Difficulty of obtaining accurate statistics.
• Movements of exchange rates make international comparisons difficult. The purchasing power within countries will always be different.
• Quality of life will vary between nations. National Income statistics will only measure material welfare [consumer goods] and not **externalities** [environmental factors] , or way of life such as climatical factors [Eg :comparing a temporate climate with a tropical climate - UK with Fiji].
• It fails to measure real wealth as the **distribution of income** will vary between countries. This is illustrated by the **Lorenz curve.**

Real and Money National Income.
• **Money or Nominal National Income** is the value of national output at **current prices.** This is the market value at any given time and makes no account for inflation. Therefore, it would be impossibe to **distinguish real changes** in **volume** from changes in **value** of output.
• **Real National Income.** This is the nominal value of output **adjusted** to **price changes.** A **price deflator** is an index used to **eliminate** the **impact of inflation.** There are two main price indices used in the UK.
  i). **The Retail Price Index [RPI].** This adjusts consumer goods and services.
  ii). **The GNP deflator.** This covers all consumer and capital goods.

The calculation of Real GNP.
This is calculated in **two** ways :
a). Real GNP = Nominal GNP   b). Real GNP = Price index of the base year.
                GNP deflator.   Price index of the current year.

John Maynard Keynes developed the ideas in his book " **General Theory of Employment, Interest, and Money** " [1936] that governments could influence the level of economic activity to achieve full employment. This was a break from the Classical economists who were more concerned with the " **distribution of income** " rather than " **income determination."**

Key National Income Terms.

Y	National Income.	**APC.**	Average propensity to consume.
C	Consumption.	**APS.**	Average propensity to save.
I	Investment.	**MPC.**	Marginal propensity to consume.
G	Government expenditure.	**MPS.**	Marginal propensity to save.
X	Exports.	**MPT.**	Marginal propensity to taxation.
M	Imports.	**MPM.**	Marginal propensity to import.
J	Injections.	**K.**	The multiplier.
W	Withdrawals.	Δ	Proportional change in.
AD	Aggregate demand.		
AS	Aggregate supply.		

Aggregate Demand.
Aggregate demand means the **total demand or planned expenditure** within the economy as a whole. This is comprised of the total of **C + I + G + (X - M).**

Components of aggregate Demand.
Consumption. (C).
This represents the **expenditure by households** on goods and services which satisfies their current wants. This is the **most important component** of AD.

The consumption function.
Keynes believed that the **level of income** [disposable income] had an important influence on household expenditure. The level of consumption has **two elements** :
• **Autonomous consumption.** This part of household expenditure does not vary with the level of income.
• **Income-induced consumption.** This is directly influenced by the level of income. There is a **relationship** between **consumption** and **disposable income**.
Therefore, the **consumption function** is expressed as follows : **C = a + bY.**
[**a** = autonomous consumption, and **b** = income induced consumption].

The propensity to consume.
• **The average propensity to consume.** (APC). This is the proportion of **total** disposable income spent on consumption.
EG :   APC $= \dfrac{C}{Y}$

• **The marginal propensity to consume.** (MPC).   This is the **additional** amount [or last £] of consumption as a result of a change in disposable income.

EG : $MPC = \dfrac{\Delta C}{\Delta Y}$

Savings. [S]
This is defined as the part of disposable income which is **not spent.**
Influences on savings.
• **The level of disposable income.**   The level of savings increases with income.
• **For a definite objective.**   For a holiday, car, or other consumer durable etc.
• **The rate of interest.**   Higher rates encourage greater savings.
• **Contractual reasons.**   An agreement with an Insurance company to pay monthly premiums for Life assurance , a Pension fund for superannuation.
• **Social attitudes.**   Attitudes of thrift, habit, feeling of security.
• **For a rainy day.** For an emergency, unemployment, sickness, car repairs etc.
• **Government policies.**   Tax incentives directly encourage savings.
• **The rate of inflation.**   High rates of inflation will discourage savings in the short term, while in the long term households will increase savings to restore living standards.

The propensity to save.
• **The average propensity to save.** (APS).   This is the proportion of total disposable income which is saved by the household. EG : $APS = \dfrac{S}{Y}$

• **Marginal propensity to save.** (MPS).   This is the additional amount or last unit / £ of disposable income which is not spent by the household as a result of a change in disposable income. EG : $MPS = \dfrac{\Delta S}{\Delta Y}$

The relationship between consumption and savings.
Consumption + saving must equal income. EG : **Y = C + S.**
Therefore, APC + APS = 1, and MPC + MPS =1. This must be true as what is not consumed must be saved.   However, as the amount of disposable income rises , consumption will also rise, but not by as much as the rise in income.   Therefore, if the APC falls as income rises, it follows that the MPC must be less than APC.

The Paradox of thrift.
If households increase the level of savings it means less consumption and eventually lower sales for firms.   Savings is a withdrawal from the circular flow of income.   As expenditure falls firms will reduce output which means less overtime, fewer workers employed, and growing unemployment.   As the circular flow contracts the size of income and savings is reduced.

Investment. [I]

This is expenditure on capital goods and changes in stock by firms. It includes items like factories, plant and machinery, as well as additions to stock of raw materials, intermediate goods, and finished products. Investment is important because it increases future output and the wealth of the economy.

Influences on investment.
• **Business confidence.** The expectation of future demand and profits.
• **The rate of Interest.** The cost of borrowing - marginal efficiency of capital.
• **Government policy.** Corporation Tax, Investment allowances and incentives..
• **The rate of technological change.** New capital equipment & technology.
• **The level of Company profits.** 60 % of investment comes from profits.

Theories of Investment.
• **The Loanable funds Theory**.
The classical loanable funds theory suggests that the rate of interest is determined by the demand and supply of capital funds. The higher the rate of interest the lower the demand for investment funds, while supply of loanable funds [savings] will increase. On the other hand if interest rates fall the demand for investment funds will increase, while the level of savings will fall.
• **The marginal efficiency of capital [MEC].**
This is the expected return or yield on capital invested. This theory relates to the Law of diminishing returns and expresses the marginal productivity of capital in terms of the rate of return or percentage yield. This is illustrated below;

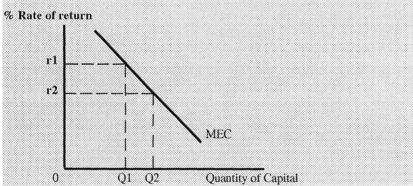

The MEC curve is the demand curve for capital as it relates to the rate of return on capital with the cost of capital. If the rate of interest falls from r1 to r2 then the expected rate of return on the firm's investment will increase. Therefore, the firm will increase its demand for capital from Q1 to Q2 This is because the cost of borrowing to finance capital spending is reduced thus making investment more profitable. Therefore, the MEC theory shows that the demand for capital equates with the cost of capital.

• **The Accelerator principle.**
This relates the level of net investment to the rate of change of national income and relates directly to the state of business confidence or future business expectations of demand. This is sometimes related to the " **Capital-output ratio** " which is the amount of capital required to produce a given amount of goods in the economy.
• If aggregate demand starts to rise faster than expected, businesses will increase investment in order to meet future demand so as not to be caught out. The increase in net investment may raise the level of national income even more sharply.
• If the level of economic activity falls, firms may delay future net investment which may cause a sharper drop in national income.
Therefore, the accelerator tends to accentuate booms and slumps of the trade cycle.

Weaknesses of the accelerator model.
• Problem of time lags as firms will wait and see if trends are long-term.
• Firms will often have spare capacity and will not respond immediately to changes in national income.
• The capital goods industry may not be able to satisfy demand.

Government. [G].
This includes expenditure by central and local governments on goods and services.
Eg : G is an injection, while T is a withdrawal from the circular flow.

Trade Net Exports. [X - M]
This represents the **international sector.**
• **Exports [X]** is an **injection** into the economy as it increases domestic output.
• **Imports [M]** is a **withdrawal** as it adds to another country's output.

National Income Equilibrium. Y = C + I + G + [X - M], or S+T+M = I+G
This is the level of income or output where planned expenditure equals actual income. The equilibrium level of national income can be illustrated by using the ideas of injections and withdrawals from the circular flow of income.
The Keynesian cross diagram.

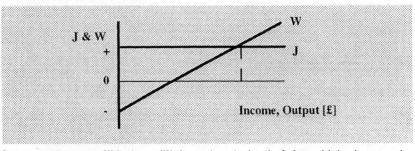

Income and output will be in equilibrium when the level of planned injections equals the level of planned withdrawals or leakages.

Disequilibrium of National Income.
• Deflationary or Recessionary gap.

This shows the extent of **spare capacity** or **unemployment** within the economy which is measured by the shortfall in output Yf - Y.

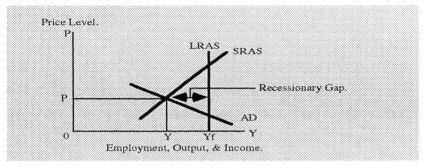

If the equilibrium level of income is at **Y** it reflects insufficient demand within the economy causing unemployment.   To close the deflationary gap the government could increase government spending [**G**], or reduce taxation [**T**] in order to stimulate aggregate demand.   Aggregate Demand rises from AD1 to AD2 to the full employment equilibrium [Yf].

• Inflationary Gap.

The diagram below illustrates a situation where the economy is operating beyond the full employment level (Y1).   This is referred to as over employment and the amount is shown by Y1 - Yf.   Firms can only increase output at current price level by increasing overtime at Yf.   Output increases from 0Yf to 0Y1.   However, in the long term the shortages in labour and other raw materials will increase costs which means the aggregate supply shifts from AS1 to AS2 to a higher price level (P1 to P2).   The shift in the aggregate supply curve illustrates the effects of **cost push inflation** - the increase in costs pushes the price level fom P1 to P2.

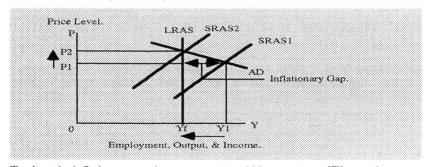

To close the inflationary gap the government could increase taxes [**T**], or **reduce** government spending [**G**] to achieve full employment equilibrium [Yf].   Aggregate demand falls from AD1 to AD2.

The Multiplier [K].

The multiplier shows how much national income changes as a result of a change from any of the components of aggregate demand. It is important to remember that the multiplier has a cumulative effect on national income or output and it works over a considerable period of time.

The **multiplier formula** is expressed as :

• **In a two sector economy** as $\quad K = \dfrac{1}{1 - \overline{MPC}} \quad$ or $\quad \dfrac{1}{\overline{MPS}}$

• **In a four sector economy** as $\quad K = \dfrac{1}{W} \quad$ or $\quad \dfrac{1}{\overline{MPS + MPT + MPM.}}$

The greater the value of MPC the greater the impact of the multiplier.
EG : As MPC + MPS = 1, and if MPC = 0.8, then MPS = 0.2. If income rises by £ 10, then consumption will increase by £ 8, while savings will increase by £ 2.
If the government increases [G] £ 500 million on public works programmes then the **multiplier process** will be as follows.

$K = \dfrac{1}{1 - 0.8\,[\,MPC\,]} \times$ £ 500 million. $\qquad$ Therefore, $K = \dfrac{1}{0.2\,[\,MPS\,]} \times$ £ 500 million.

K = 5 x £ 500 million = £ 2500 million.
Therefore, the initial government injection of £ 500 million has **increased national income** by **£ 2500 million.**

The Multiplier and economic policy.

Keynes argued that governments should use " **discretionary fiscal policy** "
[ie government spending or taxes] to influence the level of economic activity.

The Multiplier and the accelerator.

The combined effect of the multiplier and accelerator helps to explain the trade cycle. As the economy moves out of recession [ie exports may rise] an increase in investment would increase incomes and employment. The multiplier process will increase demand and output which sets off the accelerator. As the level of economic activity nears full employment the rate of growth slows down and shortages and bottlenecks occur as a result of excess demand. Prices rise faster than output making goods uncompetitive both in the domestic and overseas markets. As output falls, firms start to reduce overtime and the numbers employed. The multiplier works in reverse, this is accentuated by the accelerator. Firms will reduce future investment as the economy moves into recession.

The Trade Cycle.

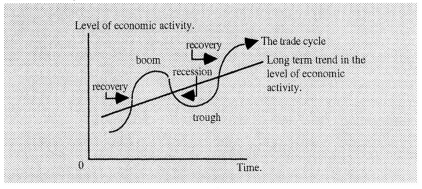

The trade cycle reflects the level of economic activity within the economy. The trade cycle measures the rate of change in economic growth or unemployment. As the economic activity moves to the top of the trade cycle it reflects increased business confidence, rising output and employment, and an increase in economic growth and incomes. However, the level of economic activity will eventually slow down as a result of the problems associated with excess demand. The trade cycle moves into recession with rising unemployment, increased business failures, and low economic growth. The **trough** or <u>slump</u> shows the bottom of the trade cycle, before the economy recovers again. The trade cycle has a duration on average of 7 to 10 years.

Explanations of the Trade Cycle.
• Internal or endogenous factors.
These are factors that occur within the economy and include the following :
a). political events, **b).** the multiplier & accelerator, **c).** business confidence.

• External or exogenous factors.
These occur outside the economy and include the following ;
a). population movements, **b).** oil crisis, **c).** wars and revolutions, d). sun-spots.

Aggregate Demand (AD).

This is defined as the **sum total of all planned expenditure in the economy**. In a simple economy aggregate demand is equal to the planned consumption expenditures.   Eg : C + I+ G+ (X - M).

The Aggregate Demand Curve.

The aggregate demand curve shows the **relationship between national income (or employment, output, and income) and the price level**.

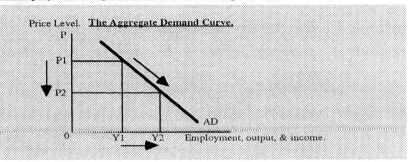

The **aggregate demand curve slopes downwards from left to right because the level of economic activity is greater at lower prices than at higher prices.**
• A decrease in the price level reduces interest rates which will increase the demand for goods and services.
• A decrease in the price level increases the real wealth of all households holding cash.   They will spend more.
• A reduction in the domestic price level increases the competitiveness of exports and reduces imports.   This means an increase in real output.

Factors influencing Aggregate Demand.
Real variables.
These are changes in planned autonomous expenditures.
• **Business confidence and Investment.**
• **Changes in Government fiscal policy.**
• **Exogenous factors influencing net exports.**

Monetary variables.
The money supply.   This shows how changes in the money supply will affect the real economy.   Changes in the money supply and its impact are referred to as the **"Monetary Transmission Mechanism"**.
Changes in the price level cause movements along the AD curve, while if any of the factors that influence real or monetary variables change then the AD curve will shift to the right or left.

Aggregate Supply (AS).

This is defined as the **sum total of all planned production in the economy.**

The Aggregate Supply Curve.

The aggregate supply curve shows the r**elationship between real output and the price level.**

Factors influencing the Aggregate Supply Curve.
• **Basic wage rates.**
• **Cost of raw materials and components.**
• **Productivity, technology, and stock of capital.**

If any of these factors change then the AS curve will shift outwards, or inwards. Although the Keynesian and Classical economists agree about the shape of the aggregate demand and the short run supply curve they disagree about the shape of the long run aggregate supply curve.

The Long run Keynesian Aggregate Supply Curve.

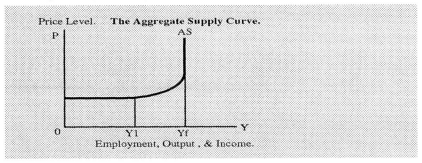

The Aggregate supply curve shows the following points.
• Up to Y1 the AS curve is shown as a flat or horizontal line. This shows **excess capacity** within the economy such as unemployment and any increase in output has no impact on the price level. This reflects **mass unemployment.**

• The AS curve between Y1 and Yf starts to rise as the amount of spare capacity diminishes. As output rises unit costs start to increase as the economy moves near the full employment equilibrium (Yf). The increase in output adds more to the price level than output. This reflects increasing bottlenecks and shortages in the economy.

• **At Yf** the AS curve is shown as a vertical line as **all resources are fully employed.** There is no excess capacity. Output cannot be increased. Any increase in aggregate demand will only result in the prices. Therefore, in the short term AS curve becomes steeper as it nears the full employment level.

57

Aggregate Demand and Supply.

The Long run Classical Aggregate Supply Curve.

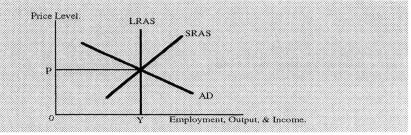

The Classical economists argue that the long run aggregate supply curve is shown as a vertical line. This shows the long run equilibrium at full employment as they believe that this is also the **natural rate of unemployment.** In the long run wages are flexible both upwards and downwards which is associated with shifts in the short run aggregate supply curve.

The Aggregate Demand and Supply Equilibrium

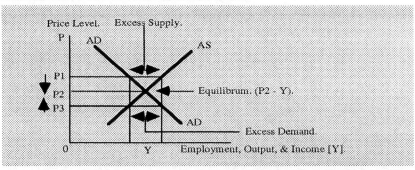

The **equilibrium** occurs when the Aggregate Demand curve intersects the Aggregate Supply Curve at the **price level P2** and the **equilibrium real national output at Y**. If prices are above the equilibrium prices and output will fall back towards the equilibrium. Similarly if prices are below the equilibrium excess demand will occur and prices and output will move back up towards the equilibrium.

58

Changes in the equilibrium.

The impact of changes in aggregate demand and supply on the national income equilibrium will depend on the economic model.

• The Classical Model.

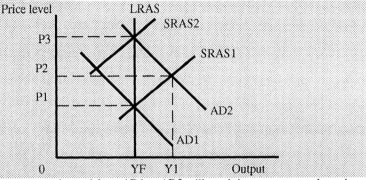

A rise in aggregate demand from AD1 to AD2 will result in a movement along the aggregate supply curve. Both prices and output will increase from P1 to P2 and YF to Y1 respectively. In the long term the aggregate supply will move inwards [SRAS1 to SRAS2] and return to the long run equilibrium [LRAS] but at a higher price level at P3. Therefore, according to the classical economists any increase in aggregate demand without a corresponding increase in LRAS is inflationary. Some economists equate the LRAS curve with the natural rate of unemployment [NRU]. The economy will always be in long term equilibrium at full employment or [NRU].

• The Keynesian Model.

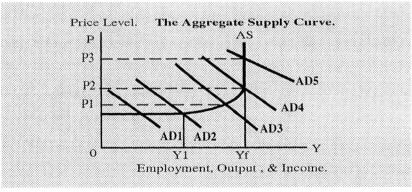

According to the Keynesian model any rise in aggregate demand will only be inflationary if the economy is already at full employment [YF]. During a recession any increase in aggregate demand [AD1 to AD2] will increase output but not prices. As the economy nears full employment the amount of "**spare capacity**" falls. Any increase in aggreagate demand will have a greater impact on prices than on output.

59

18.   Supply-Side Economics.

Supply side economics is concerned with how **changes in aggregate supply** will affect national income.   Therefore, government policy involves **micro-economic reforms** which will change aggregate supply through increased efficiency of individual markets.   Therefore, the **Aggregate Supply Curve will move outwards**.   By shifting the aggregate supply curve to the right, output and productivity will increase while the price level and natural rate of unemployment will fall.

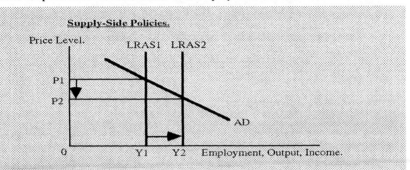

Supply-Side Policies.
This involves various micro economic reforms to improve efficiency of individual markets within the economy.

The Labour market.
These policies are designed to remove obstacles to the free market of labour ;
• Reduction in trade union power to improve labour flexibility.
• The abolition of the minimum wage.
• Reducing marginal tax rates to improve personal incentives.
• To improve the skills and training of the workforce to improve labour mobility.
• Reducing welfare and other state benefits to reduce voluntary unemployment.

The Capital market.
This involves improving competition in the capital market.
• Deregulation of the capital and money markets.
• To reduce public sector borrowing [PSBR] and the effects of crowding out.

The Goods market.
This involves improving competition and productive and allocative efficiency.
• Deregulation and privatisation in the public sector.   This has included
    - The sale of state owned assets. Eg : British Telecom, British Gas etc.
    - Contracting out of public services. Eg : refuse collection, school cleaners.
• The reduction of state subsidies to inefficient producers.
• The reduction of trade barriers to increase free trade.   This will increase competition and inward foreign investment.

Entrepreneurship.
This aims to improve the enterprise culture and incentives for small businesses.
• Reducing personal marginal tax rates, and Corporation tax [tax on profits].
• Improved labour market flexibility to improve productivity.
• Increasing the efficiency of the capital market.
• To reduce administration costs for small businesses. Eg : increasing VAT thresholds, easier planning procedures etc.

Advantages of Supply-side policies.
Fiscal policy.
Lower marginal tax rates create incentives to work hard, and encourage enterprise.
The " **Laffer curve** " shows the **relationship** between **tax rates** and **tax revenues**.

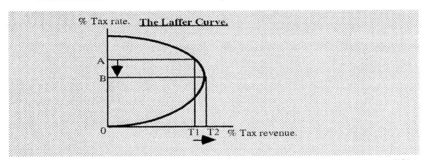

By cutting marginal tax rates [A to B] tax revenue may actually increase [T1 to T2].
Unemployment.
By increasing aggregate supply this will reduce unemployment without increasing inflation.   This is particularly true if the economy is near full employment.   There-fore, the natural rate of unemployment will fall.
Competition.
This will increase both allocative and productive efficiency.

Disadvantages of Supply-sided policies.
Unemployment.
The Keynesian economists argrue that increases in the aggregate supply curve will not reduce mass unemployment.
Increased inequality.
Supply-side policies to increase personal incentives, and measures to improve the free market and economic efficiency will increase inequalities within society.   This can be illustrated by the outward movement of the Lorenz curve.
Market failure.
Increased emphasis on the free market and a reduction in the role of the government may increase **welfare Loss** for society through the misallocation of resources.

61

19.   Employment and Economic Growth.

Unemployment is defined as those who register themselves as willing and available for work at the Department of Employment. The unemployment rate is calculated as a percentage of the working population.

Registered unemployment. x 100

Total working population.

The official figure is **seasonally adjusted** which allows for seasonal fluctuations in the unemployment figures which occurs at particular months of the year.

Full employment

This is **impossible in a dynamic economy** as there will always be a degree of unemployment such as frictional, seasonal, and voluntary unemployment. According-ing to Lord Beveridge's report in 1944, 3% unemployment was considered as full employment However, most modern governments would assume that a figure of 5 to 6 % unemployment as near full employment.   On the other hand the classical economists equate the natural rate of unemployment as full employment.

Unemployment to the level of vacancies.

This relates the number of unemployed to the number of vacancies.   If vacancies equal those unemployed it indicates full employment, while excess vacancies over the numbers registered unemployed show over employment, while excess of unem-ployed to the number of vacancies is a sign of unemployment.

Types of unemployment.

• **Cyclical or general unemployment.**   This relates to the general level of economic activity or trade cycle.   It reflects the level of aggregate demand.

• **Structural unemployment.**   This is associated with declining industries which tend to be the basic industries concentrated in certain areas - Coal, Steel industries.

• **Technological unemployment.**   This a special type of structural unemployment as industries substitute capital for labour.   Eg Robots in car factories etc.

• **Frictional unemployment.**   This is caused by workers moving from one job to another [temporarily unemployed].

• **Casual unemployment.**   This is a type of frictional unemployment where workers are out of work for short periods of time.   Eg : building or construction.

• **Seasonal unemployment.**   This is caused by seasonal fluctuations in demand such as holiday work, weather conditions in agriculture, construction industries etc.

• **Regional unemployment.**   This is unemployment concentrated in particular areas which are usually the result of structural decline of basic industries.

• **Voluntary and Involuntary unemployment.**   Voluntary unemployment is where workers are not prepared to work at present wage rates, while involuntary unemploy-ment is where workers are prepared to accept work at existing wage rates .

• **Natural rate of Unemployment.**   This is the part of the workforce which chooses voluntarily to remain unemployed when the labour market is in equilibrium.

• **Hidden unemployment.** This includes categories not included in unemployed statistics such as part-time workers such as women who do not bother to register with the Department of Employment, or school leavers or students who continue with higher education rather than registering themselves unemployed, or firms who keep skilled workers on until orders pick up in the future.

The cost of unemployment.
• Loss of output and lower economic growth.
• Loss of government revenue such as income tax, national insurance, and VAT.
• Increased government expenditure as a result of increased state benefits.
• Falling living standards and increased proverty.
• Loss of individual incomes, loss of pride and status.
• Increased stress and health problems for the unemployed and their families.
• Increased crime and social disorder.

Policies for unemployment.
• **Cyclical / General unemployment.** To increase aggregate demand by implementing expansionary fiscal policy and a loose monetary policy, and possible import controls to protect domestic employment and industries.
• **Structural unemployment.** To increase regional and occupational mobility of labour by retraining of new skills etc, and have import protection which could be phased out over a number of years.
• **Frictional / Casual unempoyment.** Improved job information and retraining.
• **Regional unemployment.** Regional policies to provide assistance for industry and job creation.
• **Voluntary unemployment.** To increase the gap between benefits and wages. To reduce the level of benefits, or reduce direct taxes and increase tax allowances, or to impose minimum wages in order to increase the incentive to work.

Economic Growth. This is defined as the increase in a country's per capita national income. Eg : GDP, or GNP. This is one of the government's key objectives to increase the output of goods and services. Therefore, over time the Production Possibility Curve will move outwards.

Methods of achieving Economic Growth.
• **To increase resources** by (i). Increased net investment, (ii). Increase the size of the Labour force, and (iii). Discover new resources. Eg : North Sea Oil / Gas etc.
• **To improve the efficiency of existing resources** by (i). Reducing unemployment, (ii). Improving Education, and Research facilities, (iii). Improving Technology and encouraging innovation to increase productivity. Eg : Improving the Skills of the work force, new machinery and methods of production.
Benefits of Economic Growth include the following : (i). Increased living standards Eg : increases in material wealth of goods and services, (ii). Increased quality of life.
Problems or Cost of Economic Growth are measured in terms of **Externalities.**

20. Fiscal Policy.

Keynesian Demand Management.
The traditional method of explaining the role of fiscal or budgetary policy is to use the Keynesian model of the economy.

Fiscal Policy.
This is simply using **government spending** and **taxation** to influence the level of aggregate demand.

The Multiplier Process.
An important feature of the Keynesian model is the multiplier effect of changes in the rate of spending on the components of aggregate demand.

Fiscal measures.
Automatic stabilisers.
These are built in adjustment mechanisms that help to stabilise the level of economic activity and they do not require any change in government policy.
These include **(i) Progressive taxation** and **(ii) Transfer payments**
• When incomes are rising and demand is increasing, a **progressive taxes** will automatically **move** incomes up the next **marginal tax bracket**. This will reduce inflationary pressures.
• In times of a recession where demand and incomes are falling a system of transfer payments also acts as a built-in stabiliser. As individuals lose their jobs they qualify for unemployment and other supplementary benefits. This means that demand does not fall as fast as employment falls.

Active or Discretionary Fiscal Policy.
This is a deliberate manipulation of government spending and taxation to influence aggregate demand to achieve various economic policy objectives. This policy was called **Discretionary demand management** and was used up to the mid 1970's.

To reduce unemployment or to close a deflationary gap.
The objective is to **raise the level of aggregate demand** and to stimulate the level of economic activity. The government may introduce a budget deficit [G>T].
• **By increasing the level of government expenditure.** As the government is the largest spender in the economy it exerts a powerful influence on aggregate demand. Any increase in government spending will stimulate further increases in consumer spending and the effects will spread throughout the economy via the multiplier.
• **By cutting taxes.** This will raise the level of disposable incomes, while reductions in Corporation tax may stimulate investment spending.
• **To increase net exports (X - M).** By granting export subsidies and imposing tariffs on imports. However, membership of the EU and GATT reduces the government's freedom to use such measures.

64

To reduce inflation or to close an Inflationary gap.
The objective is to **reduce the level of aggregate demand.** The government may introduce a budget surplus [T>G].
• **To reduce the level of government spending.** However, cuts in public spending are likely to provoke strong political opposition and cuts in capital projects are very difficult to **stop once implemented - eg :** road building, hospitals, schools.
• **To increase the level of taxation** This will reduce disposable incomes.
• **By reducing tariffs on imports** would ease the inflationary pressures, but such a measure could only be considered by a country with a very strong balance of pay ments position.

The Limitations of demand management policies.
• **Conflicting policy objectives.**
Governments in the 1950's and 1960's found it impossible to maintain a stable level of prices and low unemployment. The economy tended to move from boom to mild recession - Eg : **Stop - Go cycle.**.
• **Time lags.**
One of the problems of demand management is that it takes time to implement government fiscal changes.
• **Inadequacy of statistical data.**
This makes fine tuning of the economy almost impossible.
• **Inadequate economic knowledge.**
It is almost impossible to predict accurately the changes in economic variables.

Interpretation of fiscal policy.
Keynesian view of fiscal policy.   Neo-Classical view of fiscal policy.

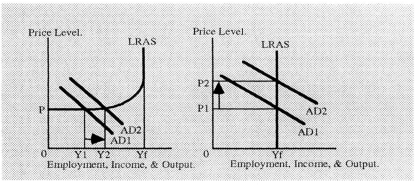

• To the **Keynesians** an expansionary fiscal policy is seen as a means of stimulating employment and economic growth especially in times of mass unemployment.
• To the **Neo-Classicalists** an expansionary fiscal policy is considered inflationary as increases in aggregate demand add more to prices than to output.

21. Rent, Interest, and Profit.

The demand for factor incomes is a **derived demand**. This means that the demand for the factors of production depends on the demand for what they can produce.

Factor Mobility.

The greater the mobility of the factors of production the more likely the economy will respond to changes in demand and adapt new ideas and technology etc.

Types of mobility.

• **Geographical mobility** is the extent to which factor resources can move from one area to another.

• **Occupational mobility** is the extent to which factors of production can be used for alternative uses.

  Land is occupationally mobile [can be used for agriculture, manufacturing, private and public construction etc], but geographically immobile.

  Labour is both occupationally [depends on skills, retraining, qualifications etc]and geographically [depends on social ties, age, costs] mobile.

  Capital will depend on the nature of the asset. The more specific the asset the more immobile it is [Eg : a blast furnace compared to a van, tools, computer etc].

  Enterprise is perhaps the most mobile of all the factors of production as it responds to changes in demand.

Rent

In economics rent is explained in terms of **opportunity cost.**

• **Economic Rent.** This is a surplus payment over and above the minimum supply price or opportunity.cost.

• **Transfer earnings.** This is the minimum payment or opportunity cost to keep the factor employed in its present use.

• **Quasi rent.** This is a short term economic rent as a result of a shortage of supply for a particular factor Eg : accountants, or prime office space etc.

• **Pure economic rent.** This is a reward for any factor which is perfectly inelastic in supply. Eg : famous entertainer, professional sports person, a brilliant barrister, or a prime site in a city centre etc. All its earnings will be economic rent.

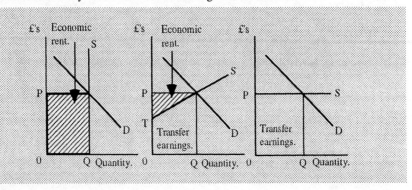

Diagram **(i)** illustrates the idea of **pure economic rent** as the supply of a factor is totally inelastic. **Diagrams (ii)** and **(iii)** show that over time the level of economic rent will disappear as factors will be attracted by the surplus payments over and above the minimum. In the long term all factors will earn the minimum as the supply increases. This example applies to all the factors of production.

Interest.

Interest is seen as a reward to the lender, and a cost to the borrower.
The rate of interest includes the following factors :
• It is a reward for the loss of liquidity.
• It covers the risk of possible default.
• It compensates for a fall in the value of the currency as a result of inflation.
• It covers the cost of administration in collecting the repayments.

The Classical Funds Theory. Under this theory the equilibrium rate of interest is determined by the supply of loanable funds from savings, and the demand of loanable funds for investment.

The Liquidity Preference Theory. Keynes argued that the rate of interest is determined by the two following factors.
• The Stock of money.
• Households desire to hold money in a liquid form or liquidity preference which is influenced by the propensity to consume, and the propensity to save.
Liquidity perference. This is determined by three factors.
• **Transactions motive.** Money is used to buy every day goods and services.
• **Precautionary motive.** Money is kept in reserve for emergencies.
Eg : unexpected bills etc. It is kept in a liquid or near liquid form.
• **Speculative motive.** Once the first two motives have been satisfied a person or investor will only release funds if it yields a good rate of return or interest. The demand to hold money varies with the rate of interest, the higher the rate of interest the greater the cost of holding money in a liquid form.

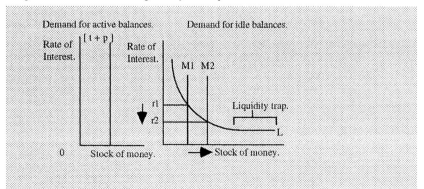

The demand for active balances reflects the transactions and precautionary motives which is not really influenced by the rate of interest, while demand for idle balances illustrates the relationship between speculative motive and the rate of interest. The rate of interest is that which equals the demand to hold money. If the stock of money is set at M1 then the rate of interest is determined at r1. If the stock of money is increased from M1 to M2 then the rate of interest falls to r2.

The Liquidity trap. This occurs if the rate of interest is **so low** that individuals prefer to hold onto their money as everyone expects interest rates to rise in the future.

Changes in the demand and supply of money.
1). **Change in the demand for money.**   2). **Change in the supply of money.**

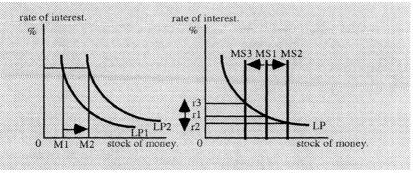

• The liquidity perference curve will shift if **real incomes** or **prices change.**
• The money supply shifts in accordance with **government monetary policy.**

Profit.
This is the reward for enterprise which covers the risk of uncertainty and organising the other factors of production. The idea of economic rent can be applied to profit. Normal profits is regarded as transfer earnings, while economic rent is considered as abnormal profits.
The characteristics of profit include the following :
• It is a residual reward as profit cannot be anticipated in advance.
• It can be negative as an entrepenuer may incurr losses.
• It fluctuates over time in response to demand and the costs of production.

Importance of profit.
• It stimulates innovation, and efficiency of production.
• It is a major source of business finance as 60 % of profits are reinvested.
• It allocates resources as high profits reflect consumer demand and attract resources from other declining industries.
• It encourages individuals to set up businesses and take the risk of uncertainity.

Wages are the payments made by an employer for the use of labour. Wages are the price of labour. It is a general term which covers many different types of payments which include wages and salaries [time rates or day rates], as well as piece rates, fees, commission, and profit sharing.
• **Nominal Wages.** This is the basic money wage.
• **Earnings.** This includes the basic or nominal wage plus all other additional payments such as overtime, bonuses, shift allowances etc.
• **Real Wages.** This has been adjusted to inflation.
• **Wage Drift.** This is the difference between national awards and local negotiations at a regional or factory level which account for local factors in order to attract additional workers. This will include additional payments, fringe benefits .

The marginal productivity theory
This is based on the " **Law of diminishing returns."**
• **Marginal physical product. [MPP].** This illustrates the additions to total output with the employment of each extra worker. In other words its productivity.
• **Marginal revenue product. [MRP].** This shows the addition to total revenue of employing each additional worker.

Assumptions of the marginal productivity theory.
• Perfect competition in the product market.
• Prefect competition in the labour market.
• Labour is homogeneous or identical.
The Marginal productivity of a factory. employing workers on a production line.
Price of product = £ 10, Cost or Wage of worker = £ 40. MRP = Price x MPP.

Numbers employed.	Output	MPP.	MRP.
1	6	6	60
2	13	7	70
3	25	12	120
4	35	10	100
5	43	8	80
6	50	7	70
7	56	6	60
8	60	4	40
9	63	2	20
10	64	1	10

If the price of the product remains constant as the firm expands output the
MRP = MPP x price. Therefore, the firm will employ 8 workers as the cost of the 8th worker equals its revenue which is £ 40.

Wages and Trade Unions.

The importance of the MRP Curve.

The MRP curve represents the demand curve for Labour. If the cost of wages rises the demand for labour will fall. The demand for labour will shift when there is a change in demand for the final product, or when labour becomes more or less productive. The slope of the MRP curve depends on the elasticity of demand for labour.

a). A rise in the price of Labour.   b). A shift in the demand for labour.

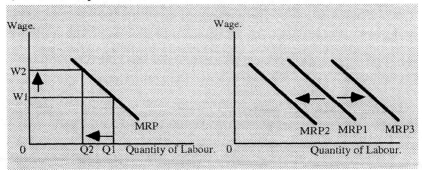

Criticisms of the marginal productivity theory.
• Difficulty in measuring the output of service workers [teachers, doctors etc]
• Fails to allow for distortions in the Labour market caused by Trade Unions.
• Fails to allow for different skills and attitudes of different workers.

The Demand for labour.
The demand for labour is determined by three things.
• The demand for labour is a **Derived Demand.** This means that the demand for labour depends upon the demand for the final product.
• **Its productivity.** Labour will only be demanded if it can increase the firm's profits by increasing production. This is illustrated by the **"marginal physical product "** [MPP] which is related to the **law of diminishing returns**. As extra workers are employed, total output, or total physical product increases. However, MMP, will increase up to a point and then it will start to decline in accordance with the law of diminishing returns.
• **Its marginal revenue product [MRP].** This is the additions to total revenue [P x MPP] from employing an extra unit of labour. This is the demand curve for labour. An employer will employ additional workers until its MRP = cost [or MC].

The determinants of the elasticity of demand for labour.
This is influenced by;
• **Time.** The longer the time period, the easier it is to substitute labour.
• **The ability to substitute labour with other factors.** [ie **capital** for labour].
• **The proportion of labour costs to total costs**.
• **The Elasticity of demand for the final product.**

70

Supply of Labour.

The supply of labour in the economy is influenced by the following factors ;
• **The size of the total population.** This will determine the size of the labour force or working population. This includes, age distribution, [birth, death, & migration], sex ratios, labour laws etc.
• **The mobility of labour.** This covers occupational, and geographical mobility.
• **Trade Unions.** The relative strength and organisation of Trade Unions.
• **The net advantage of Labour.** This involves the trade off between work and leisure. This is illustrated by the regressive or backward bending supply curve.

Specific factors affecting supply of labour for a particular occupation.

• **Pay** - higher paid occupations will attract more workers than lower paid ones.
• **Income in kind** - perks, and fringe benefits etc.
• **Conditions of employment** -dangerous, unpleasant conditions, anti social hours.
• **Types of employment** - status, job satisfaction.
• **Qualifications and training** - Skilled to unskilled workers.
• **Trade Union membership** - A closed shop will restrict supply.

Wage Determination.

In theory wages are determined by the interaction of demand and supply for labour.

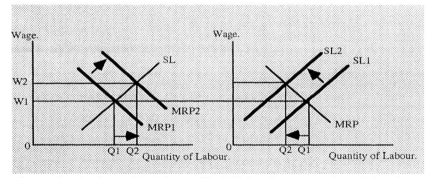

• **Increasing the demand for labour**. Trade Unions increase the demand for labour by increasing productivity, supporting an advertising campaign, by overmanning agreements etc. Therefore, the number of workers employed rises.
• **Decreasing the supply of labour.** Trade Unions restrict the supply of labour by imposing a closed shop, insisting on long apprenticeship periods, or higher qualifications etc. Therefore, the number of workers employed falls.

Wage differentation.

• Labour is not homogenous which is characterised by its diversity [ie age, skills].
• Labour is not perfectly mobile which is reflected by regional wage rates.

71

Perfect and Imperfect Labour Markets.
Perfectly competitive labour markets.
In a perfectly competitive labour market there are a large number of small firms hiring a large number of individual workers.
• The demand curve for labour, MRP, is downward sloping.
• The supply curve of labour [MC of labour] is perfectly elastic. The firm will hire any number of workers at the existing industry wage rate. [diagram a) below.]

Imperfectly competitive labour markets.
An imperfectly competitive labour market is one where :
• The firm is a dominant or monopoly buyer of labour - a **Monopsony.**
• The firm is faced by a monopoly supplier of labour, like a **trade union.**
This is shown in **diagram b).** below.

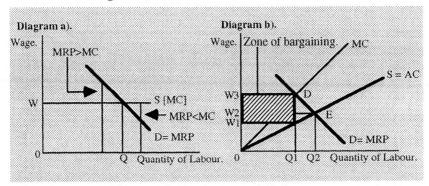

Diagram a). In a **perfectly competitive labour market** the supply curve for labour is perfectly elastic. The equilibibrium wage rate OW which is the wage rate for the whole industry. In a perfectly competitive labour market MC = AC as the cost of labour is constant. The profit maximising firm will employ OQ workers at a wage rate of OW, where MRP [D] = MC [S] of labour.

Diagram b). In an **imperfect labour market** the firm will employ workers where MC = MRP of labour [OQ1]. However, the monopsonist will only need to pay OW1 to attract OQ1 workers. Therefore, the **monopsonist will employ less labour and pay a lower wage than in competitive markets.**

Trade Unions and the Labour Market.
• **A trade union is an organisation which represents the collective interests of its members.** The most important function of a trade union is to increase wages and improve working conditions of its members.
• **Collective bargaining** is a process by which unions and employers negotiate pay and working conditions either at a national or local level.
• **Professional Associations.** This represents the interests of professional employees such as Doctors, Dentists, Accountants, Solicitors etc.

Trade Unions - A monopoly supplier of Labour.
Many trade unions operate in the labour market where there are monopsony employers - a sole seller of labour, the trade union negotiating with a sole buyer of labour, the monopsonist. Eg : TGWU negotiating with a Car Manufacturer.

The bargaining power of trade unions.
The trade union has the power to increase both wages and employment levels compared to a situation without a union. The extent to which it can do both depends on the relative strength of the union. The diagram above shows that it can increase both the wage rate and employment up to Q3, or point Z. This because the monopsonist still has,a profit incentive to hire extra workers so long as the **MRP > MCof labour.** If wages are increased beyond Z, it will only be at the expense of some of the workers already employed which will be between points X and Z or 0Q3 to 0Q1.

The power of Trade Unions.
• Trade Union membership and militancy.
• The demand curve for labour is relatively inelastic.
• Profitability of the employer.
• Government legislation.

Causes of labour market failure.
Mobility of labour. In a perfect market, there is complete mobility of labour. In reality there are many obstacles to mobility.
Segmented labour markets. This suggests that there is little movement between labour markets. This is based on the idea of the **dual labour market.**
• **Primary labour market** is often unionised, most workers are employed by large employers such as oligopolistic or monopoly firms or by government. They are better paid, and qualified.
• **Secondary labour market** is characterised by non-unionised workers, are employed by small firms, and the workers they tend to be in low skilled or unskilled occupations on low pay.
Trade Unions and Monopsony employers often create unemployment in the labour market.
Government policy. Government measures such as taxation on goods, interest rate policy, health and safety legislation, equal pay, minimum wages will affect the labour market.

Correcting labour market failure.
• **Minimum wage legislation.** Until recently wage councils had the power to fix wage rates in low wage industries - retailing, catering, and garment manufacturing.
• **Equal pay legislation.** This aims to raise wage rates of workers who perform work of equal value. Eg : woman and workers from ethnic minorities.
• **Health and safety legislation.** These measures improve working conditions.

73

23.   Money and Inflation.

Money, Wealth, and Income.
• **Money** is the medium of exchange which is used to buy everyday commodities.
• **Wealth** is a stock of assets held at any given time :
   i).   financial assets - cash, bank deposits, shares, and insurance policies etc.
   ii). Physical assets such as property, antiques etc.
• **Income** is a flow of money over a period of time- monthly salary.

Functions of money.
• **Medium of exchange.** It is accepted in the exchange of goods and services.
• **Measure of value.** It allows for the measurement of goods and services by using prices to reflect their value.
• **A store of value.** It means that money can be saved and used later.
• **A standard of deferred payment.** This allows the use of credit since repayments can be repaid at a future date in fixed money terms.

Characteristics or Qualities of money.
• **Acceptability.** The most important characteristic as individuals agree to its use.
• **Divisibility.** It can be broken down into smaller units - £ 10, £5, £1, 50p, 20p.
• **Portability.** It is easy and convenient to carry around.
• **Durability.** It last a long time.

The nature of money.
Money is defined in terms of **liquidity,** the ease of converting an asset into cash.
Liquidity. This is the degree to which an asset can be converted into cash without capital loss.
• **Money.** This consists of notes and coins and has intrinsic value but is legal tender, and Bank deposits which consist of entries in a bank ledger.
• **Bank Deposits**. They consist of **(i) Demand deposits / sight** [current accounts] and **(ii) Time deposits** [savings accounts]. They are regarded as money as they act as a store of value and a medium of exchange as well as being used in the settlement of a debt. Bank deposits are used to settle 90 % of all transactions in terms of value.
• **Near money or Quasi money.** These include financial assets such as Building society accounts etc. They have a degree of liquidity but may have a period of notice. They act as a **store of value** but not as a medium of exchange unless a cheque can be drawn against the account.
• **Money substitutes.** This covers things like credit cards since they are used as a medium of exchange but cannot be used as a store of value, since it merely delays the settlement of a debt.

The Money Supply.
The money supply is the **stock of liquid assets** which is used for the exchange of goods and services. The problem with the money supply is one of definition.

• **Narrow money**. This includes **liquid money assets** and is primarily used as a medium of exchange. This includes **M0**. [notes and coins], and M2 [M0 + retail deposits of the banks and the building societies].

• **Broad Money**. This also includes **less liquid money assets** which are used as a store of value. It includes M4 [M2 + deposit accounts held by the banks and building societies], and M5 [M4 + plus the private sector holdings of money market instruments]. M1 and M3 are no longer used.

The relationship between bank deposits and the money supply.
There is a direct relationship between the growth of the money supply and the creation of bank deposits. Bank lending is important for three reasons :
• It helps to finance household and business expenditure.
• It is the most profitable part of the commerical banks' activities.
• It has a direct influence on the money supply.

Credit Creation.
This is a process by which the commercial banks are able to create money or new bank deposits. The example below shows how the banks are able to increase the initial deposit of £100 to £1000 assuming a 10 % cash reserve ratio.

Stage 1.		Stage 2.	
Liabilities.	Assets.	Liabilities.	Assets.
Deposits £100	Cash £100	Deposits £100	Cash £10
			Advances £90
£100	£100	£100	£100
Stage 3.		Final Stage.	
Liabilities.	Assets.	Liabilities.	Assets.
Deposits £90	Cash £9	Deposits £1000	Cash £100
	Advances £81		Advances £900
£90	£90	£1000	£1000

The Credit creation process. This process depends on the following assumptions :
• All money deposited at the banks is lent out in accordance with the credit ratio.
• The money lent by the banks is spent by its customers.
• That all the money spent returns to the banking system.
The **size** of the **credit** or **bank multiplier** depends on the **cash ratio.** The higher the ratio the lower the value of the credit multiplier and vice versa.
The **credit multiplier** can expressed by the following formula :
Eg ; If the credit ratio = 10 %, and the original deposit is £ 500 then :
The credit multiplier = $\underline{1}$ x 100 = Total increase in bank deposits.
$\qquad$ R [cash ratio]
Eg : $\underline{1}$ x 100 = 10 x £ 500 = £ 5000 = Total increase in bank deposits.
$\quad$ 10

75

Money and Inflation.

The Functions of the Bank of England.
The bank of England is the **Central Bank** and is at the centre of the money market.
• **It issues Bank notes in England and Wales.** It prints, distributes banknotes.
• **It is the governments Bank**. The Exchequer Account records Tax revenues and current government expenditure, while the National Loans Fund maintains all government borrowing and lending.
• **It manages the foreign exchange and gold reserves**. It administers the Equalisation Account.
• **It is banker to the other banks.** It administers inter-bank settlements.
• **It is Lender of last resort.** It maintains the liquidity of the banking system.
• **It implements the governments monetary policy.** This is perhaps its most important function which involves controlling the level of economic activity and maintaining the government's monetary economic objectives.
• **It supervises the financial system in the UK**. It issues licences to banks and trys to prevent fraud by financial institutions.
• **International Role.** It represents the government on international bodies like the IMF.

The Financial Markets.
The Money Market. This is concerned with **short term** borrowing.
The Capital Market. This is concerned with **long term** borrowing.
The Stock Exchange. A market for the **issue** of **new** and **second hand shares.**

Inflation.
Inflation is defined as a **rise in the general level of prices and a corresponding fall in the value of money.**

Theories of inflation.
The **Quantity Theory** shows a direct relationship between the money supply and the general level of prices. The theory states that **MV = PT**. This is known as the **Fisher Equation.**
M = stock of money, V = velocity of circulation, P = average price level, T = number of transactions of goods and services. This theory links changes in the money supply to the level of economic activity. As V and T are assumed to be constant in the short term any change in M will mean an increase in P. However, it is more useful to change this equation to MV = PY Here, Y = total value of real output. PY represents **money GDP.** However, both equations state a basic truism, that both sides of the equation must be equal. Therefore, if V and Y are fairly stable over the short term any change in M will result in a change in P. The result is a very powerful equation since it can be used to predict the general level of prices or inflation. The equation can be rearranged to become P =M x $\frac{V}{Y}$

The theory suggests that the source of excess demand is the result of increases in the money supply. In other words " **Too much money chasing too few goods.**"

Types of Inflation.
• **Creeping or Mild inflation.** This is very low rates of inflation. Eg : 0-3%
• **Runaway or Hyperinflation.** This is a very rapid increase in prices which are out
of control as experienced in Germany in 1923, and more recently in Russia.
• **Suppressed inflation.** This occurs when governments impose price controls to
control inflation as with a price and wages freeze. However, this delays the problem
since once the restrictions are lifted prices and wages rise rapidly as in the 1970's.
• **Stagflation.** This is a situation of high inflation and high unemployment.
• **Slumpflation.** This is like stagflation but with negative economic growth.
• **Imported inflation.** This is the result of rising prices of imported raw materials,
components, and other goods and services. Eg : Oil crisis 1973, 1979.

Measurements of Inflation.
• **Retail Price Index. [RPI].** This measures consumer goods and services.
• **Producer Price Index. [PPI].** This measures input prices at the factory gate.

Causes of Inflation.
Demand Pull inflation.

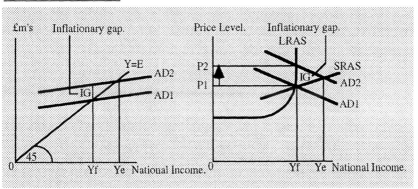

This is where aggregate demand excedes aggregate supply and this is sometimes
referred to as a situation where there is " **too much money chasing too few goods.**"
The excess demand pulls up prices from AD1 to AD2 and as the economy is operating at full employment prices rise. This is shown as an **inflationary gap.**

Causes of Demand pull inflation.
• Private citizens using past savings, and obtaining credit to finance spending.
• Increased government borrowing [PSBR] financed by printing more banknotes, or
from the banking sector, or from overseas sources [fixed exchange rate].
• Increased exports which increases domestic income, but reduces the quantity of UK
produced goods.
• Increased capital or defence goods whose opportunity cost is a reduction in
consumer goods.

77

Money and Inflation.

Cost push inflation.

This is caused by rising production costs such as wages, raw materials, power, and transport.   Therefore, firms pass on the increased costs in higher prices.   As prices rise this may trigger a **Wages spiral** as workers demand increases in wages to match the rise in prices.   As costs and prices rise the SRAS curve moves inwards from SRAS1 to SRAS2 to SRAS3.   Output, employment, and incomes fall as firms become less competitive.

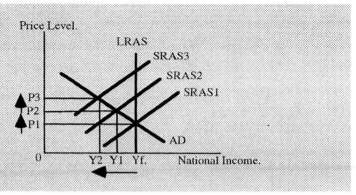

Wages Spiral

Rising costs may cause a wages - price spiral.   A rise in consumer prices causes trade unions to demand at least a similar percentage rise in wages in order to protect their members real incomes and living standards.   Usually producers will concede to the trade union demands and will pass on the increase in wages onto the consumer in the form of higher prices.   The wage - price spiral is increased as unions include **"future inflationary expectations"** into their negotiations.   Prices rise still faster.

Causes of Cost push inflation.

• Labour shortages and trade unions are in a postion to increase real wage rates.
• Increasing production by increasing overtime.   Wage costs rise.
• Shortages of raw materials and components.   Eg : Oil Crisis.
• Firms conceding to trade union demands in order to avoid a prolonged industrial dispute which may result in a financial loss through falling sales and market share.

The Effects of Inflation.
• **Redistribution of Income**.
Those on fixed incomes [salary earners, pensioners] are worst off as the value of money falls, compared to those on commission, fees, or dividends.   There is also a redistribution of income from savers to borrowers, and from non unionised to unionised labour.
• **Production and Employment**.
Mild inflation may encourage output and stimulate growth as profit margins rise.

78

However, a **rapid inflation** undermines competitiveness, business confidence. Output and employment will fall, while in the long term the economy may collapse and political unrest may increase.

• **Balance of Payments.**
Inflation reduces and undermines exports and makes imports more competitive in the domestic market having an adverse effect on the Balance of Trade. There will be a long term impact on the exchange rate.

• **Government finances.**
In the **short term** mild inflation may help the government : **i).** As a major borrower the **cost of debt servicing** is reduced in real terms., **ii).** Tax revenue may increase because of **fiscal drag** as households incomes rise into higher marginal tax brackets, as well as increased revenue from Corporation tax and VAT.
In the **long term** rapid increases in inflation cause real economic problems,

  i). Unemployment and lost output.
 ii). Balance of Payments problems.
iii). Social and political instability.

Controlling Inflation - Aniti - inflationary policies.
The type of policy will depend upon the causes of inflation.

Control of Demand-Pull inflation.
This requires a reduction in planned expenditure to a level that will purchase full employment output at constant prices. To close an inflationary gap aggregate demand must fall to the full employment equilibrium.

• **Monetary Policy.**
This increases the cost and reduces the quantity of loans available to the public. By restricting the money supply or the price of credit [interest rates] it becomes more difficult to finance expenditure using borrowed money. Such a policy is called a **tight monetary policy.**

• **Fiscal Policy.**
This increases taxes (T) and reduces government expenditure (G). The net result is a budget surplus as the government withdraws more money from the economy than it injects through its own expenditure. The level of aggregate demand is reduced as purchasing power is reduced throughout the economy.

Both monetary and fiscal measures used together in a **deflationary policy** is aimed at reducing spending power in the economy.

Control of Cost-Push inflation.
The deflationary policies above may indirectly reduce cost push pressures as a fall in aggregate demand for goods and services will create unemployment. This will reduce the bargaining power of trade unions.

79

• **Prices and Incomes Policy.**
This attempts to prevent incomes (ie wages and dividends) pushing up prices, by ensuring that wage increases are only matched by increases in productivity. Such a policy was used in the 1960's and 1970's and were of two types :
   i). **Voluntary.** The government seeks the co-operation of trade unions and employers to limit wage and price increases.
   ii). **Statutory.** In this case the rules of the incomes policy are enforced by law.

• **Supply-side Policies.**
These are policy measures to increase aggregate supply in the economy. Supply-side policies are aimed at reducing overall costs and inflationary expectations within the economy.
In the long term supply-side measures according to the classical economists, will increase output and employment by improving efficiency and productivity. There-fore, production costs fall with corresponding improvements in competitiveness.

The Phillips Curve.
The Phillips curve shows a **trade-off between inflation and unemployment**.

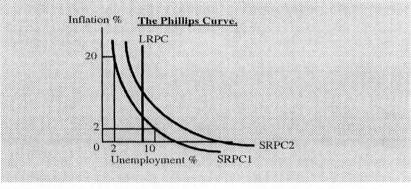

The diagram shows the relationship between % rate of inflation and % level of unemployment. Therefore, if inflation was 2 %, unemployment would be 10 %, or if inflation was 20%, unemployment would be 2%. The Phillips curve has been revised since the 1960's as most economies have experienced stagflation or slumpflation. The Phillips curve has moved outwards which means it takes a greater degree of unemployment in order to reduce inflation [SRPC1 to SRPC2].
In the long term the Phillips curve [LRPC] is represented as a **vertical line** as it equates with the " **natural rate of unemployment.**" The classical economists believe that any policy that attempts to reduce unemployment below the natural rate of unemployment will result in higher inflation in the long term as the economy returns to its equilibrium [LRPC].

80

24.   Monetary Policy.

Monetary policy is defined as a set of measures to influence the level of aggregate demand by influencing the money supply or the price of money [rate of interest] or any other monetary variable to achieve various economic policy objectives.
Eg : Price stability.

The importance of the money supply.
The "monetary transition mechanism" shows how changes in the money supply have an impact on the price level and the level of national income.

High powered money or monetary base.
This simply means cash and includes ;
• Notes and coins held by the banks.
• Operational balances held at the Bank of England.

Importance of high powered money or monetary base.
This sets the limit to the amount of deposits that can be created by the commercial banks. As the amount of notes and coins in circulation cannot be restricted, operational deposits at the Bank of England perform a key role in the implemenation of monetary policy.

Monetary Policy targets.
To achieve various macro -economic objectives [ie stable prices] the government may set targets. Eg : **The Medium term Financial Strategy.** The idea is to impose economic discipline on monetary policy.   Targets can be set for the money supply, as well as for public spending, and the PSBR.

Types of monetary policy.
Tight monetary policy.
The monetary authorities aim to curb inflation and reduce the the level of economic activity by increasing interest rates, or by reducing the money supply.
Loose or easy monetary policy.
This aims to increase the level of economic activity such as increasing employment or economic growth by reducing interest rates, or by increasing the money supply.

Monetary objectives in the UK.
The monetary authorities in the UK have two main objectives.
• **Short term interest rates.**
To ensure that short term interest rates are kept stable from day to day in the money markets [ie Treasury Bills and Money at Call or Short Notice].
• **The PSBR.**
To raise money to finance government expenditure.   In recent years the government has attempted to reduce the size of the PSBR by reducing public expenditure.

Monetary Policy

• **Other monetary policy objectives.**
   The money supply.
Since 1976 governments have set money supply targets. Initially M1 and M3 were targetted, while in 1985 M0 replaced M1 as a measure of narrow money.
   The exchange rate.
Up to 1971, and between 1990 and 1992 [membership of ERM] the government has been committed to maintaining a fixed exchange rate by buying and selling pounds.
At other times, and since the ERM crisis the pound has been allowed to float and find its own level. However, interest rates have been used to influence the pound.

Bonds, bills, and interest rates.
Bonds. These are long term government loans which earn interest. They are sometimes referred to as gilt edged stock.
Bills These are short term loans and they are a form of IOU as they promise to pay the bearer a sum of money at a specific time in the future [ie 3 months].
• **Commercial bills.** These are issued by private companies.
• **Treasury bills.** These are issued by the government.
The greater the amount of discount for a bill, the higher the rate of short term of interest in the money market.

Instruments of Monetary Policy.
   The Bank of England is responsible for implementing the monetary policy.
Open market operations.
This involves the **buying and selling of government securities** which will affect the money supply and interest rates.
• If the Bank of England sells government bonds the money supply will contract and interest rates will tend to rise. The sale of bonds will reduce the banks cash ratios and to restore their cash balances they will be forced to reduce their ratio of liquid assets to total deposits. Therefore, to restore their liquid balances the banks will be forced to reduce bank lending to total liabilities.
• If the Bank of England buys government bonds the money supply will increase and interest rates will tend to fall. This will increase the banks deposits and therefore increase the banks ability to lend in the form of advances.
The Discount rate.
This is the rate which the Bank of England uses to calculate the price it will pay for bills and bonds as lender of last resort.
The discount rate is linked to the bank base rate. This is the key interest rate in the economy. All other interest rates are linked to the base rate.
• If the discount rate rises bank rates and other rates are likely to increase.
• If the discount rate falls bank rates and other rates are likely to fall.
• The higher the discount rate is set above market rates, the greater the potential loss by the commerical banks. To increase their cash reserve ratio to total assets the banks will be forced to reduce their total assets or deposits. This will reduce the money supply. If the discount rate is set below market rates the opposite will occur.

Funding.
This refers to the **replacement of short term debt by long term debt.** By issuing more long term securities it reduces the commmercial banks liquid assets and thereby reduces their ability to lend.
Over-funding. This is designed to increase long term interest rates as the government sells more securities than it needs to the non banking sector to finance the current PSBR.
Monetary base control.
The amount of bank lending is set by the amount of **"high powered money."** In theory the monetary authorities have a powerful way of influencing the level of the money supply. However, this has never been used in the UK as this would result in large movements in short term interest rates as the money markets respond to day to day cash balances.
Other Bank of England measures.
• **Special deposits.** These are compulsory loans to the Bank of England which are frozen at zero rate of interest. This will reduce the banks liquid assets and they were used in the 1960's and 1970's.
• **Supplementary deposit scheme.** This is sometimes called **"the corset".** The Bank of England would impose interest rate penalities or fines if bank deposits overshot their limit. By restricting bank deposits the monetary authorities were able to control the growth of the money supply. This was used in the 1970's.
• **Direct controls.**
    i). **Quantitive controls.** This sets limits on the volume of bank lending.
    ii). **Qualitative controls.** This involves requesting the banks to direct lending to particular customers such as exporters, or businesses instead of personal customers.
• **Moral suasion.** The banks may be asked to change their lending activities.

Limitations of monetary policy.
Disintermediation.
This means that the banking system as a financial intermediary between borrowers and lenders has been by-passed. Therefore, disintermediation makes it difficult for the financial authorities to measure and control the money supply. The banks have found ways around various government controls.
• **The growth of parallel markets.** These are outside Bank of England control.
• **Borrowing " Off shore. "** Eg : borrowing from New York, or Frankfurt.
• **Practice of on-lending.** This makes quantitive controls too difficult to enforce.
• **Exploiting loopholes in monetary regulations.** This might involve switching assets with other financial institutions.

Monetary policy constraints.
The money supply, the rate of interest, the PSBR, and the exchange rate are all interlinked. However, the government cannot control all these monetary variables at any one time as it faces a **"trade off "** as it can only fix one of these variables at any one time.

83

The basis of trade.
If countries specialise in commodities which enjoy a **natural** or acquired **advantage** then trade would benefit all trading countries in lower prices and increased output.

Advantages of Trade.
• It increases the variety of goods.
• It enables countries to obtain goods they cannot produce themselves.
• It encourages specialisation, economies of scale, and greater efficiency in response to foreign competition.
• It encourages countries to specialise in the products for which they are best suited.

Theories of International Trade.
The theories of Absolute and comparative advantage show how world output can be increased through specialisation and trade.
• **Absolute Advantage.**
A country has an absolute advantage when it can produce a commodity more efficiently per resource unit than its trading partners.
• **Comparative advantage.**
This is when a country has a lower opportunity cost in producing a commodity than its trading partners.

Assumptions of Absolute and comparative advantage.
• **No trade barriers to trade.** This means free trade between countries.
• **Perfect factor mobility.**
• **No transport costs between the trading countries.**
• **There are Constant returns and constant average costs of production.**
• **All resources are fully employed.**

By using the principle of absolute and comparative advantage the example below illustrates the advantages of trade.
We also assume that there are only two countries. Each country has equal resources and uses its half of its resouces between the output of cars and trucks.

Table 1

Trading Country.	Cars units.	Trucks. units
Country A	30	15
Country B.	5	10
Total world trade.	35	25

Table 1 shows that Country A has an absolute advantage in both commodities with a comparative advantage in cars. Country B has a comparative advantage in trucks since it can produce 1 truck compared to 0.5 of a car with the same resources. If both countries specialise in the commodities in which they have a comparative advantage world output would be as follows.

Table 2.

Trading Country.	Cars units.	Trucks. units
Country A	60	0
Country B.	0	20
Total world trade.	60	20

Table 2 shows an increase in car production but a small drop in truck output.
If Country A decides to produce both commodities but to still specialise in cars in which it has a comparative advantage.

Table 3.

Trading Country.	Cars units.	Trucks. units
Country A	50	5
Country B.	0	20
Total world trade.	50	25

Table 3 shows that world output has increased compared to table 1. The examples also illustrate each country's **opportunity cost ratio** which is **2 : 1** for Country A and **1 : 0.5** for Country B. Trade will only be advantageous for both countries within this ratio. It shows the __Terms of Trade__ between the two countries.

__The Terms of Trade.__
The Terms of Trade is an index of export prices divided by an index of imported prices. The index is calculated as follows :

The Terms of Trade = Index of export prices x 100
                     Index of import prices

• A favourable movement has export prices rising more rapidly than import prices.
• An unfavourable movement has import prices rising more rapidly than export prices.
Therefore, a favourable movement indicates that the value of exports will rise relative to imports. If things remain equal this will improve the Balance of Trade or Merchandise Trade. However, it is possible to have a favourable movement on the Terms of Trade and an Unfavourable Balance of Trade (and vice versa). This is because a rise in export prices may reduce the volume of export sales. This will depend on the **elasticity** of demand for Exports and imports.

__Arguments against Free Trade or Protectionism.__
• __To protect infant industries__   To allow new firms to grow and get established.
• __To protect employment__   To allow industries to adjust to structural decline.
• __To protect the Balance of Payments.__   To reduce a trade deficit.
• __To prevent dumping and unfair competition.__
• __To protect key strategic industries__ . Eg such as agriculture, defence, energy.

85

Methods of Protection.
• **Tariffs or customs duties.** This is simply taxes on imports. A tariff is either **specific** - a set amount. Eg £ 2 per item, or **ad valorem** - set % of the value per item.
• **Quotas.** This sets a restriction on the number of imports by issuing licences.
• **Subsidies.** This helps exporters by reducing costs such as export credits etc.
• **Exchange Controls.** This restricts the use of foreign currency for imports.
• **Administrative controls.** This uses administrative procedures, and documentation or **"red tape"** to restrict imports.
• **Voluntary agreements.** This is an agreement between governments.
• **Embargoes.** This a complete or partial ban on trade or goods.

The impact of Tariffs and Quotas.

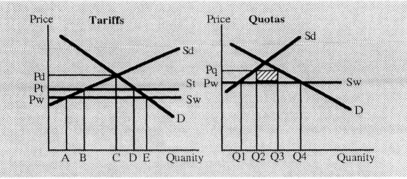

Tariffs. If the world price of a good is Pw, the imposition of a tariff will shift the supply curve upwards to St. Domestic demand will fall by DE, while domestic output will increase by AB. Imports will fall from AE to BD.
Quotas. The introduction of a quota will reduce supply and increase the domestic price from Pw to Pq. Demand will from Q4 to Q3, while domestic output will increase from Q1 to Q2. Importers will make a windfall gain which is shown by the shaded area above.

Multilateral Trade agreements.
General Agreement on Trade and Tariffs. [GATT].
The role of GATT is to promote international trade and cooperation by reducing trade barriers. Originally it covered manufactured commodities, but with the completion of the " **Uruguay Round** " which started in 1986 it also includes **a).** agriculture, **b).** textiles, **c).** services, and **d).** copyrights and patents.

World Trade Organisation [WTO].
In 1993 the Uruguay Round was finally concluded in the GATT Accord. A new permanent World Trade Organisation [WTO] was created to replace GATT, and it was given greater powers to reduce protectionism.

Bilateral Trade agreements.
Trading Blocks.
The are two main trading blocks.
• **Free Trade Area.** This removes tariffs between member countries but each
country is allowed to set its own tariff with the rest of the world. Eg : NAFTA. CER.
• **Customs Union.** This removes tariffs between member countries, but all member
nations have a common tariff with the rest of the world. Eg : EU.
• **Organisation of Petroleum Exporting Countries. [OPEC.]**   This is a suppliers
organisation or cartel of oil producer nations which meet to set a common price of
oil.

The European Union [EU].
This is a customs union and was originally set up in 1956 and was known as the
European Economic Community [EEC].   There are now 15 member sates, although
this may be extended to other countries of Eastern Europe.   The immediate aim of
the EU is the creation of a single market, while the long term goal is the creation of a
political and monetary union.

Advantages and disadvantages of EU Memebership .
Advantages.
• Businesses will have free access to markets which would otherwise be protected by
tariffs and quotas.
• UK firms have a larger market to sell their goods.   Eg: The EU is the largest free
market in the world with a potential of 380 million customers compared to 58
million.
• Businesses operating within the EU are protected from foreign competition.
• Increasesd opportunities for economies of scale, and joint ventures, or mergers with
other European businesses.

Disadvantages.
• UK businesses are no longer free to buy goods, raw materials and components from
the lowest cost producers around the world because of the common external tariff.
• European firms will have free access to the UK market and increased competition
will reduce market share for UK businesses.
• The external tariff protects businesses from world competition which could reduce
the incentive to improve and innovate products, and reduce costs.
• UK businesses will have to adapt their marketing strategies, organisational struc-
tures, and communication systems to suit the needs of customers in individual
member states.   Costs are likely to rise.

• **The Common Agricultural Policy [CAP].**
This policy was designed to increase agricultural output, stabilise markets and
guarantee supply, and to give farmers a reasonable standard of living.   This was to

be achieved by setting minimum prices for all agricultural products, and farmers could then choose to sell their produce on the open market, or to the EU at the minimum or intervention price. They were also protected from overseas competition by a complex system of tariffs and quotas. This has resulted in overproduction and surpluses which has been very costly for the consumer, and the taxpayer, as well as to efficient agricultural countries such as Australia and New Zealand.
The recent reforms of CAP, and the recent GATT agreement has reduced the subsidies given to farmers. This will have a major impact on agriculture and related businesses. It will also mean that smaller farmers will be forced out of business.

* **Single European Market.**
This came into existence at the beginning of 1992. It removed other barriers to free trade such as differing product standards and legislation which favoured domestic producers. The Single Market means greater **harmonisation** between member countries of the EU. The advantages include ;
• Lower administative costs for producers.
• Removal of border controls, and technical regulations - reduced transport costs.
• Increasing economies of scale and rationalisation as a result of strategic takeovers and mergers within Europe. Such mergers will these organisations to compete effectively in a globle market. Eg : BMW and Rover.
• Increased inward investment as Europe becomes more competitive.
Eg : From the Far East.
• The Free movement of resources such as Labour and Capital.
• Increased competition within EU particularly in areas of Public procurement.

* **Regional Development.**
The European Regional Development Fund provides funds to help relieve unemployment and encourage development projects in poorer parts of the EU.
• The retraining of workers to learn new skills.
• Finance and grants to firms who set up in these areas. Additional assistance may be provided by the **European Social Fund.**

* **The Social Chapter.**
The **Maastricht Treaty** attempted to harmonise working conditions throughout the EU by the **Social Chapter** which included;
• A minimum wage.
• A maximum working week of 48 hours.
• A minimum of four weeks paid holiday a year.
• The freedom to join a trade union.
• The right to be consulted and informed about company plans,
• Protection for young workers.
• Proper and adequate training.
The UK government obtained an opt-out clause because it believed thar labour costs would rise making UK firms less competitive, thus discouraging foreign investment.

26.   Balance of Payments.

The Balance of payments **records all financial transactions between the UK and the rest of the world.** It is a measure of Britain's competitiveness with the rest of the world.

The Current Account.
• **The Balance of Trade or Merchandise Trade.**
This records the **value of all physical goods** exported and imported and includes primary products, raw materials and components, and manufactured products. This is known as the **Visible Balance.**
• **The Balance of Invisibles.**
This records the **value of services** exported and imported and includes items such as tourism, transport, financial services such as banking and insurance, profits and dividends (ie International investment income) and gifts (ie Transfers). This is known as the **Invisible Balance.**

The Capital Account.
This records changes in Britain's **overseas assets** and **liabilities.**
Capital inflows.
This is the movement of funds into Britain.
Eg : A Japanese Firm buying a UK business inside Britain.
Capital Outflows.
This is the movement of funds out of UK.
Eg : A British. firm buys a factory overseas.
The two main components of the Capital account are as follows :
• **Short-term flows.**
These are simply movements of money since they are not involved in the creation of a physical asset. These include the purchase of Treasury bills, or commercial bills, or a simple deposit in a UK bank account. This type of capital flow is very volatile and responds to changes in interest rates and exchange rates. This is referred to as **speculative or hot money.**
• **Long-term Flows.**
This involves the creation of a physical asset such as a direct investment by a British firm that buys an overseas business, or a portfolio investment by an Insurance company of overseas shares. This also includes governments transactions such as UK government contributions to the EU budget.

The Balancing Item.
This makes an allowance for errors in Balance of Payments calculations.
Overseas Reserves.
This is a surplus of foreign currencies and Gold reserves, and foreign government securities held by the British government. These can be used to correct a Balance of Payments deficit, or to support the exchange rate.

89

Balance of Payments.

Overall Balance.

This is simply the Current account and the Capital account added together, and with the balancing item equals the **total currency flow.** This will give a Surplus or Deficit. In the end the overall balance must always **equal zero** since it shows how a Deficit was financed or what happened to a Surplus. This is known as the balance of official financing.

Disequilibrium on the Balance of Payments.

• In the **short term** a deficit can be financed out of the foreign currency reserves from past surpluses, or by borrowing.
• However, in the **long term** a large **surplus** as with Japan , or a large deficit will become a major problem and requires action..

A Long term Deficit on the Balance of Payments.

This depends on the nature of the deficit.
• If the deficit is on the **Capital account** this is not a real problem. As British firms invest overseas it will in future years return as profits and dividends on the Current account as a positive flow inwards as invisible earnings.
• If the deficit is on the **Current account** this is more serious as it shows that the country's goods and services are uncompetitive in international markets. Although the country will experience a welfare gain in the short term as the country consumes more than it produces it has to be financed out of the currency reserves or by borrowing. The reserves will eventually diminish.

Policies to correct a Balance of Payments deficit.

This will depend on the **exchange rate mechanism.**
• Under a **Floating exchange rate** the uncompetitiveness will be corrected by the foreign exchange market since the currency will depreciate in value. Exports will regain their competitive edge while imports will become more expensive. The Balance of Payments moves into equilibruim.
• Under a **Fixed exchange rate** the country will have to adopt the following measures in order to correct the disequilibrium.
    i). **Import controls.** This will involve a combination of **Tarrifs, Quotas,** and possible **administrative controls**.
    ii). **Exchange controls** to reduce the outward flow of foreign currency.
    iii). **Deflationary policies** to reduce the level of aggregate demand in order to encourage firms to export to compensate for the loss of sales in the domestic market, and to reduce consumer demand for imports.
    iv). **Devaluation.** The currency is pegged to a **lower rate of exchange** making exports more competitive and imports more expensive against its trading partners.

Problems of a Balance of Payments surplus.

• A large and persistent surplus on the Current account will cause the exchange rate to rise which may be reinforced by speculative infows on the Capital account.

90

This will reduce the competitiveness of exports while making imports more competitive.   In the **long term** domestic firms may invest overseas causing de-industrialisation of the economy and rising unemployment.
• A rise in exports may cause **demand-pull inflation.**
• Under a fixed exchange rate a surplus will increase the **money supply.**

Policies to reduce a Balance of Payments surplus.
Again this will depend on the exchange rate mechanism.
• Under a Floating Exchange Rate the currency will appreciate in value thereby reducing the surplus and the Balance of Payments disequilibrium.   Exports will be reduced while imports increase.
• Under a Fixed Exchange Rate a surplus will be reduced by the following :
   i). Reduce import controls and encourage imports.
   ii). Encourage invisible imports such as holidays abroad etc.
   iii). Encourage Capital outflows; transactions, foreign investment, overseas aid.
   iv). Revaluation to increase the value of the currency at a higher exchange rate.

The Marshall Lerner Condition.
This shows the importance of **price elasticities** for both **exports** and **imports**, and states that a fall in the exchange rate will improve the Balance of Trade if the " **sum of the price elasticities for the demand of exports and imports is greater than unity.**"   Therefore, the volume of exports must rise as export prices fall and the volume of imports must fall as import prices rise.   However, if exports are more elastic, and imports more inelastic the Balance of Payments may actually deteriorate.

The " J " Curve Effect.
The " J " **Curve** shows that the balance of payments may actually **deteriorate** between points after an initial devaluation before it starts to improve to the new demand and supply conditions in the long term.   The Balance of Payments may continue to deteriorate from a **loss of confidence** resulting in a **net capital outflow** of funds.   The " J " curve will move to the right.

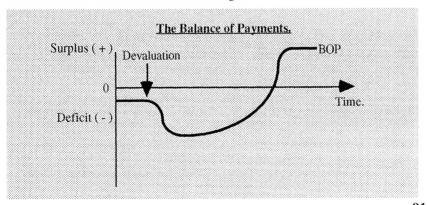

91

The exchange rate is the **price at which one country's currency can be exchanged for another in the foreign exchange market.** There are basically two types of exchange rate systems 1). **Floating Exchange rates,** and 2). **Fixed Exchange rates.**

Floating Exchange Rates.

This rate of exchange is determined by the **forces of demand and supply** in the foreign exchange market **without government intervention.**

• **Demand for £'s.** The demand for £'s arises from the need of overseas countries to buy British exports or foreign countries to invest in the UK.

• **Supply for £'s.** The supply of £'s comes from British importers for goods and services produced abroad.

a). **The Equilibrium Exchange Rate.**   b). **Changes in the Exchange Rate.**

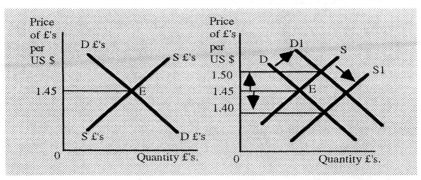

Diagram (a) shows the equilibrium rate of £ 1 = US $ 1.45.   As the demand for £'s equals the supply of £'s the Balance of Payments must also be in equilibrium.
Diagram (b) illustrates a change in the equilibrium rate.   The increase in demand [D1 to D2] shows an increase in demand for exports D £'s>S £'s so the currency will rise or **appreciate** in value.   If imports rise S £'s>D £'s for £'s so the currency falls or **depreciates** in value to the new equilibrium.

Fixed Exchange rates.

Under a fixed exchange rate system **the government sets the external value of the currency.** An exchange rate is maintained in value by **direct intervention** by the **Central Bank** in the foreign exchange market.
The diagram shows the agreed equilibrium rate of exchange of £1 = $1.45.   If the demand for exports rises [D to D1] a shortage of £'s will develop between A to B.   The Central Bank will be forced to intervene in the foreign exchange market and sell £'s in order to restore the equilibrium rate.   However, if imports rise the supply of £'s will increase [S to S1] in the foreign exchange market the Central Bank will be forced to buy the excess of £'s between **A** to **B** using its foreign exchange

92

reserves to restore the equilibrium

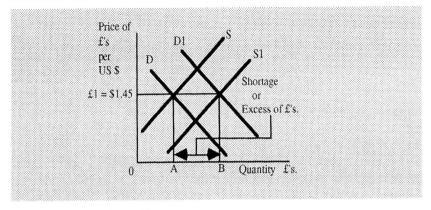

Types of Fixed Exchange Rates.
• **A fixed exchange rate or par value.** This is maintained at a particular rate of exchange or " **par value** " by the government.
• **A pegged system.** The currency is linked to a particular currency [US $], or a " **basket of currencies** " of major trading partners.
• **Adjustable peg.** The rate of exchange is linked around an agreed par value but may be changed at the discretion of the monetary authorities [ie to appreciate or depreciate].
• **Crawling peg.** This is like the adjustable peg but the rate can move away from the par value in small movements to allow for different inflation rates between trading partners.
• **Managed Flexiblity or a Dirty Float.** This is like a floating exchange rate, [a clean float], the government intervenes unofficially to maintain exchange rate targets.
• **European Monetary System [EMS].** This is a form of crawling peg where member countries keep their exchange rates within specified bands against each other. Each currency is allowed to fluctuate within an agreed upper or lower limit such as a 2.5 % movement between the Franch Franc and the German Mark. This requires the cooperation of member Central Banks to maintain agreed rates. However, the EMS has weakened since September 1992 by international speculation.

Advantages and Disadvantages of floating and fixed exchange rates.
Floating Exchange rates.
Advantages.
• TheExchange rate and Balance of Payments are always in equilibrium.
• The government is free to pursue its domestic policy objectives.
• It has no impact on the money supply.
• There is no need to keep large amounts of currency reserves as they are free to be put to more productive uses.

93

Exchange rates.

Disadvantages.
• It can increase speculation.
• It is difficult to set future export and import contract prices as currency prices fluctuate. This increases business uncertainty.
• There is no economic discipline on domestic economic objectives.

Fixed Exchange Rates.
Advantages.
• It increases business confidence as future exchange rates are known in advance.
• It imposes economic discipline on economic policy objectives.

Disadvantages.
• Speculation increases if the market believes that the currency is over or under valued.
• Maintaining the agreed par value can increase unemployment and reduce output for deficit countries.

International Liquidity.
This is maintained by the use of the following assets to settle international debts.
• Foreign currency reserves.
• Gold.
• Borrow from the IMF. Eg : Reserve positions.
• Special Drawing Rights [SDR's] issued by the IMF.

International Organisations.
• **International Monetary Fund [IMF].**
This was set up following the " Bretton Woods " agreement in 1944. Its principle aims were to **(i).** Restore international stability in world trade, and **(ii).** To help member countries with Balance of Payments difficulties, and **(iii).** To maintain stability in international exchange rates

• **The World Bank.**
This is to help developing countries with financial assistance with capital projects such as improving infrasructure, agriculture, and industry.

Monetary Union [EMU].
One of the long term aims of EU is to establish a common currency. The Maastricht Treaty stated that member countries could move forward towards monetary union if all countries meet certain **"convergence criteria"**. Eg : That interest rates, inflation rates, budget deficits, and exchange rates are in line with each other.
Convergence Criteria.
The Maastricht Treaty laid down a timetable for full monetary union membership by 1999. The new currency the "Euro" would be legal tender in 2002. Before member countries could join they had to satisfy the strict "**convergence criteria**." The

94

convergence criteria were a **set of economic targets** which had to be met for at least two years. These include;
Inflation.
Inflation rates must stay within 1.5% of the average rate in the lowest 3 countries within the EU. Countries with higher inflation rates would normally increase interest rates. This would make it difficult to maintain a stable exchange rate. Under a free floating exchange rate the currency would depreciate.
Interest Rates.
Interest rates must be no more than 2% of the average of the 3 lowest countries within the EU. This will reduce speculative capital inflows, which could de-stabilise exchange rates.
Fiscal Deficit.
Government budgets must be no more than 3% of GDP, and the national debt must be less than 60% of GDP. Countries with higher levels of borrowing [PSBR] will have higher rates of interest rates, which could de-stabilise exchange rates.
Each currency must be locked into a narrow band of the ERM for at least two years.
Advantages of the Single Currency.
• One common currency would increase trade and specialisation. This is a logical extention of the Single Market. It will create the largest free trade area in the world.
• It would reduce business costs in terms of currency transactions.
• It would increase business confidence because there would be no need to worry about exchange rate movements.
• It imposes economic discipline on all member states within the **"euroland"** as the new European central bank will ensure price stability as it will be responsible for implementing European Monetary Policy. The new central bank will be independent and would administer monetary policy for the benefit of the whole of "euroland".
Disadvantages of the Single Currency.
• Countries will not be able to devalue their currency in order to regain a competitive trade advantage.
• The loss of control over monetary policy and the partial loss over fiscal policy makes it difficult for governments to pursue other economic objectives and solve problems like structural unemployment. This could de-stabilise some of the outer regions of the EU.
• To regain a competitive edge countries will need to cut wage rates in order to compensate for membership of the single currency.
• The European Bank will set a common interest rate throughout "euroland". This could cause economic and social problems between member states. Eg : High interest rates to reduce inflation in Germany and France, might be unsuitable if there is a recession in the UK. Therefore, member countries must have similar "trade cycles". In the past the UK trade cycle has always been at a different stage to that of continental Europe.
• A common monetary policy will lead to a common fiscal policy. This could be the next step towards political union or federal europe.

95

28. Public Finance.

This covers **all public sector finance and expenditure by Central, Local government, and the public corporations.**
The Budget is central to public finance and is presented by the Chancellor of the Exchequer The Budget has **two key functions** :
• It is a **financial statement** since it is an account of government expenditure and revenue for the past financial year as well as estimates for the coming financial year.
• It is also an important **instrument of economic policy.** An overall budget surplus or budget deficit has an important influence on the level of aggregate demand and therefore the whole economy.   In this role the budget is known as the regulator.

Types of Budgets or Budgetary policy.
Macro economic role.
Budget Surplus. Here budget estimates of government revenue exceed its estimates of expenditure.   This causes a leakage from the circular flow [T>G].
• It reduces the level of aggregate demand by reducing household purchasing power.
Here a budget surplus is used to close an inflationary gap and reduce demand pull pressures.
• A budget surplus will reduce the demand for imports and help the Balance of Payments and maintain the par value of a fixed exchange rate.
• A budget surplus can be used to reduce part of the Public Sector Borrowing Requirement [PSBR].
Budget Deficit. Here budget estimates of government expenditure exceed its estimates of revenue.   Therefore, giving an injection into the circular flow [G>T].
• It increases the level of aggregate demand by increased household expenditure.
This type of budget is used to close a deflationary gap by stimulating output investment, and employment [via the multiplier].
• A deficit has to be financed by borrowing and has implications for the size of the PSBR, interest rates, and the money supply.
• It is likely to increase imports as the level of aggregate demand nears full employment as aggregate demand exceeds Aggregate supply.
Neutral Budget. The government has a balanced budget [T=G].   The aim is to control the level of government spending and thus the PSBR.

Micro economic role.
The budget can be used to influence different sectors of the economy.
• A reduction in direct taxes will encourage incentives and enterprise.
• Increases in direct taxes can be used to redistribute income and wealth.
• Increases in excise duties on cigarettes, alcohol, petrol can be used to discourage consumption on health and environmental reasons.
• It can impose import controls to protect the Balance of Payments.
• The government can direct its expenditure to key areas of the economy such as construction, roadbuilding or railways, small businesses, public utilities etc.

Government Revenue - Taxation.
The Canons of Taxation. These are the **principles of taxation** which were set by
Adam Smith in his book the Wealth of Nations in 1776.
• **Certainty.** The taxpayer must know the amount, method and time of payment.
• **Convenient.** The payment of tax should be as convenient as possible [PAYE].
• **Economical.** The collection of tax should be as cost effective as possible.
• **Equitable.** The tax must be seen to be fair for all sections of the community.

Structure of taxes.
• **Progressive.** The burden of taxation increases with income and wealth.
Eg Income tax, Capital gains tax.
• **Proportional.** The burden of tax remains the same regardless of income.
Eg : Corporation tax.
• **Regressive.** The burden of tax takes a higher proportion of lower incomes compared to higher incomes. Eg : VAT.

Types of Taxes.
• **Direct taxes.** These are **levied on income and wealth** usually at source and paid
to the Inland Revenue Department. The main types include :
(i). Income tax, on individual income, **(ii).** Corporation tax, on company profits,
(iii). Capital gains tax, on the value of assests, **(iv).** Inheritance tax, on income and
wealth at time of death, **(v).** Other taxes include, motor vehicle licences, stamp
duties.
• **Indirect taxes.** This is **taxed on spending or expenditure** and is paid to the
Customs and Excise Department. They are either **specific taxes** [a fixed money
value ie £ 2 per unit], or **ad valorem taxes** a % value of the commodity]. The main
types include : **(i).** VAT, **(ii).** Excise duties are specific taxes on domestic or imported
production such as petrol, wine or whisky, **(iii).** Customs duties are ad valorem taxes
on imported goods.

The Incidence of taxation. This shows who bears the burden of taxation.

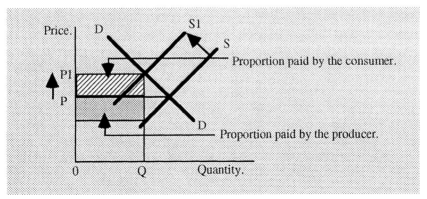

97

If the elasticity of demand is inelastic it is possible for the producer to pass on a greater amount of the burden of the tax to the consumer, on the other hand if demand is elastic the producer has to absorb the majority of the increase in tax.

Taxation policy.
Taxes are levied for several reasons.
• To raise revenue for the provision of government goods and services.
• To redistribute income and wealth.
• To regulate the level of aggregate demand.
• To encourage incentives and enterprise.

Public Expenditure.
This is grouped under the following headings.
• **The provision of public goods.** This covers services called public goods which private firms are unwilling to provide such as armed forces, the judiciary, the police.
• **The provision of social services.** The largest part of public expenditure such as health, education, and social services-pensions, unemployment, sickness, maternity, benefits etc.
• **To improve industrial efficiency**. This either provides government funds to private firms such as grants, and tax allowances, or taking key industries under public ownership.
• **To influence the level of economic activity.** This uses public expenditure to influence aggregate demand either to increase or decrease economic activity.

Borrowing.
If government **expenditure exceeds** its **revenue** then it must borrow to cover the **Budget deficit**. The difference comes under the heading of the **Public Sector Borrowing Requirement [PSBR]**. The PSBR is the amount the government needs to borrow for the **year ahead** as outlined in the budget. It is financed in two ways.
• **Short term.** The sale of Treasury bills [less than 90 days.].
• **Long term.** The sale of Bonds or Gilts [more than 90 days.].

The impact of the PSBR on the money supply.
The impact of PSBR will depend on how it is financed.
• **The private non-banking sector.** This has a neutral effect on the money supply.
• **The banking system.** There is an increase in the money supply.
• **Overseas sector.** The money suppply will increase under a fixed exchange rate.
• **Issuing notes and coins.** The money supply will increase. This is protentially very inflationary.

The National Debt. This is the total accumulated past borrowing of the government. It represents the amount owed by the government to its citizens, and to overseas institutions.

• **Internal debt.** This is held by UK citizens and institutions.
• **External debt.** This is held by overseas residents and institutions.

The burden of debt.
It is argued that the burden of debt is simply transferred from past generations to the present and future generations as past generations lived beyond their means.
This ignores the following points.
• If the borrowing is used productively to finance capital projects that increase future output then living standards then it benefits society.
• Government borrowing takes the form of securities which have a fixed rate of interest. Therefore, in real terms the value of debt is falling over time.
• Interest payments and principle repayments are met by the present generation out of taxation. Although this involves an opportunity cost of lost public expenditure elsewhere it is really a transfer of funds from taxpayers to bond holders. There is neither a loss or a gain for the community as a whole.
• The burden of debt really falls on the generation at the time of the borrowing as government expenditure was greater than its tax revenue.

Internal debt v External debt.
The external debt must be repaid out of future export earnings. As interest payments and principal repayments are transferred overseas out of export earnings then it is a loss of domestic earnings, unless the overseas borrowings increase national output by more than the cost of borrowing.
The internal debt is not a problem unless taxes are increased to cover the cost of borrowing. This may have a disincentive effect on households and firms. It may also have an impact on domestic interest rates at the time of the borrowing and result in the **"crowding out"** of private investment.

29. Managing the Economy.

Government Economic objectives.
All governments try to achieve the following objectives. However, these **objectives conflict** so the government has to **balance** these **conflicts**.
- **To maintain price stability** [ie keep Inflation within acceptable limits].
- **To maintain full employment.**
- **To protect the Balance of Payments.**
- **To ensure a fair and equitable distribution of income and wealth.**
- **To promote economic growth.**
- **To conserve and ensure the efficient use of resources for future generations.**

Conflict of economic objectives.
A **policy** for **full employment** with **economic growth** will often **conflict** with **low inflation** and a **balance of payments equilibrium.** As economic growth rises and unemployment falls, overall incomes are likely to increase. The increased purchasing power of households will increase demand, and if supply cannot be increased, prices will start to rise as well as demand for imports. The result is a **policy clash** as the **fiscal** and **monetary policies** to achieve **price stablity** and **overseas solvency** are the **opposite** to those to achieve **full employment** and **economic growth.**

Policy Instruments.
Fiscal Policy or Budgetary Policy. This uses **taxation** and **government expenditure** to control the **level of aggregate demand.**
Monetary Policy. This controls the level of economic activity by influencing the **money supply, interest rates,** the **PSBR,** or **the exchange rate.**
Other policy instruments
- **Prices and Incomes.** Policy to control incomes or wage levels and prices in order to reduce cost push pressures.
- **Balance of Payments Policy.** Import controls, and subsidies for exporters in order to reduce a trade deficit.
- **Exchange Rate Policy.** To maintain a fixed exchange rate, or exchange rate target under a floating rate by using interest rates etc.
- **Regional Policy.** This tries to influence the location of industry and employment in depressed areas of high unemployment.

Economic Policy problems.
- **Economic policy objectives cause conflicts.** Eg : Inflation v Employment.
- **Time lags** between identifying the problem and implementing policy decisions.
- **Lack of accurate statistical information** which is usually out of date.
- **Too many variables** such as world trade, demand, money supply, and exchange rates which are difficult to predict and to control.
- **Political constraints** from voters, trade unions, employer organisations, and possibly other governments and institutions [EU].

100

Government Macro Economic Policy.
Governments have a range of policies to achieve their economic objectives.

Fiscal Policy
This policy uses **government spending and taxation** to influence the level of economic activity or aggregate demand. This is sometimes called **budgetary policy.**
• **Taxation.** This influences the amount of money that individuals and businesses spend on goods and services.
• **Government Spending**. As the government is the biggest spender in the economy it has a big impact on aggregate demand. Government spending can public work schemes also tends to be more labour intensive.

Monetary Policy
This policy aims to control the **money supply** in order to influence the level of **credit spending** within the economy. As 90% of transactions of value in the UK are settled by bank deposits, bank deposits are an important component of the money supply. The Bank of England is responsible for implementing monetary policy on behalf of the government. The size of the money supply within the economy is influenced by;
• **interest rates** in the money markets - ie the price of money.
• **the amount of credit** provided by banks to its customers -Loans, & overdrafts.

Supply-side Policies.
Supply-side policies aim to encourage competition and incentives for individuals and businesses to work harder and to innovate. These measures include;
• Reducing marginal tax rates on businesses and individuals in work in order to increase incentives and innovation.
• Reducing state benefits and minimum wage controls to reduce unemployment.
• Encouraging competition in the goods and financial market by privatisation, and deregulation, and by removing trade barriers against foreign competition.
• Encouraging enterprenuership by reducing administrative controls & taxes.
• Reducing reduce trade union power in order to increase labour flexibility.

Balance of Payments and Exchange Rate Policies.
The aim of these two policies is to maintain an equilibrium on the balance of payments. A balance of payments problem exists when a country persistently has a trade deficit or surplus over a long period of time. Eg : Exchange rate target.

Managing the Economy.

Government Micro Economic Policy.
Regional Policy.
This policy aims to reduce **regional unemployment** as the result of structural unemployment, and the de-industrialisation of the UK economy.
There are two types of policies a government can adopt;
• **Take the workers to the work**. This aims to increase the mobility of labour.
Eg : Retraining and travel and relocational grants.
• **Take the work to the workers.** This aims to encourage firms to relocate into areas of high unemployment - development, and assisted areas, or enterprise zones.
Government incentives include grants and tax breaks on new investment projects.

Industrial Policy.
This policy is aimed at particular industries and businesses and includes;
• Privatisation, or the sale of government assets to the private sector. Eg : The sale of British Telecom, British Airways, the public utilities Electricity, Gas, & Water companies during the 1980's.
• Deregulation and the removal of barriers to competition. Eg : financial deregulation -allowing building societies become banks, or the reduction of red tape and bureaucratic controls, removal of trade barriers to encourage foreign competition.
• Contracting out of public services to the private sector ie parts of the Civil Service.
• Imposing market discipline on the public sector. Eg : NHS Trusts.

Competition Policy.
Economic theory highlights the benefits of competitive markets. However, the economies of scale allow monopolies, and oligopolies to become anti-competitive.
The government aims to increase competition by reducing barriers in particular markets or industries. A government will investigate;
• The market structure of individual industries - Is it a monopoly or oligopoly.
• The conduct and operation of individual firms in that market - The possibility of collusion between firms
• The efficiency of these firms and the whole industry - The level of innovation and incentives to reduce costs and use available resources efficiently.
• To ensure the public interest in respect to prices, guarantee of supply, employment.

Monopolies and Mergers.
The Monopolies and Mergers Commission [MMC] may investigate situations where;
• A single firm or producer has 25% of the market - national or local market.
• A merger of firms control 25% of the market, or where the merger takes over more than £70 million in assets.

Restrictive Practices.

Under the Restrictive Practices Act 1956 a restrictive trade practice is deemed to be any agreement between producers regarding prices, output, or the condition of sale of a product. Any such agreement has to be registered with the Director General of Fair Trading. The Competition Act 1980 allowed other anti-competitive practices to be investigated such as price discrimination, or predatory pricing - selling below cost.

Competition policy in the European Union.

European Competition Law under the Treaty of Rome applies to all member states.
• Articles 92-94 ban all government aid to firms, or industries which could distort competition.
• Article 85 bans restrictive practices which restrict markets output &prices.
• Article 86 bans firms from using its dominant position to impose unfair terms on suppliers, retailer outlets, and consumers.

30.   Index.